Last one out, turn off the lights!

GW00320437

A Migrant's Tale

Mike & Alexandra Cole

Proud to live and work in New Plymouth, New Zealand;
THE BEST CITY IN THE WORLD!

- Awarded First place and 2 Golds in the UN endorsed "International Awards for Livable Communities" (for cities of population up to 75,000).
- Awarded top city in NZ; North and South magazine, New Zealand 2008

"BRITS NZ - HELPING TO MAKE YOUR MOVE COMPLETE"

ISBN 978-0-473-14604-7

Cover design by Derek's Darkroom, New Plymouth.
Printed by Zenith Print.
Assisted by PublishMe, New Plymouth, New Zealand.
www.publishme.co.nz
Proofreading and editing services supplied by Lesley Scott.
Lel.scott1@gmail.com

Last one out, turn off the lights!

A Migrant's Tale

DEDICATIONS

This book is dedicated to those we still very much love but who are no longer with us. Each of you has been an inspiration and throughout this journey we have believed and felt that you were with us in spirit:

Lee & Ivy Cole

Bill Sugars

Alan Worrall

This is Mike's book and so the dedication is also his, but I want to make a little dedication of my own – to Mike himself.

I once said to him, "Thank you for my life – I love it. We're so lucky" and he told me that it wasn't luck, but sheer hard work that brought us to the happy stage we're now at. So much of that hard work was done by him and without his foresight, dogged determination and good humour, our move simply wouldn't have taken place.

I don't tell Mike nearly enough how much I appreciate how hard he works for BritsNZ; all the trips back to the UK and the work he does here. All that has allowed me to make New Zealand my home and has assisted me in growing and changing and becoming so much stronger and more confident a person, able to deal with everything our exciting new life may throw at us.

This emotional, funny, loving and generous man is a wonderful husband and father and to him, I just want to say, "Thank you!"

Alex Cole.

ACKNOWLEDGEMENTS

This book would not have been possible without the love and courage displayed by my family, so to Alexandra, Joseph, Jacob and Gabriella huge respect and boundless, endless, unconditional love to you all – you all rock my world!

To Lel Scott our friend, fellow migrant and proof-reader extraordinaire who has read, altered and chased us again and again to get this book done – you are an absolute star and you have our total respect and heartfelt thanks. You have very much been a major driver to get this done and we thank our lucky stars we asked you to be involved!!!!!! (Too many exclamation marks, I know, but on this occasion very well deserved.)

We must make mention of our key business partners. The Directors of Paragon Insurance (NZ), PSS International Removals (UK), Halo Financial Services (Currency Exchange, UK), National Bank (NZ), ASB Bank (NZ) and lastly (but by no means least) Outbound Media (UK) – you are all amazing people/organisations to work with and have been there with us as we built our business and new lives - thank you!

Thanks also must go to Emigrate TV who allow me to act as a roving reporter and who always offer constructive comments – thanks for all your help over the years – it has been of massive importance to us! (www.emigratetv.com)

"BRITS NZ - HELPING TO MAKE YOUR MOVE COMPLETE"

FOREWORD

I first met Mike Cole and his family back in 2003 when he, rather rashly, volunteered to take part in a unique reality documentary I was making called the *Emigrate Challenge*. The idea was that six families would each keep a video diary showing their emigration experience over a 12-month period – warts and all. What we didn't tell them was that a panel of migration experts would be secretly viewing all their tapes and casting judgment over how each family was faring.

I have to confess, I didn't hold out too much hope for the Coles. I'd had dealings with another family emigrating to New Zealand a few years earlier and, frankly, they'd been a bit of a dead loss, neither filming very much nor, it seemed, preparing adequately for their new life. Mike and Alex Cole could not have been more different. Despite frequent setbacks, disappointments and the almost inevitable emotional blackmail of certain family members, they showed the grit and determination which is the hallmark of all achieving migrants. They researched thoroughly; explored alternative avenues when any road seemed closed to them; kept positive yet realistic at all times. Once in New Zealand they threw themselves wholeheartedly into the community, getting involved in all aspects of local life and quickly setting up a help group called BritsNZ, which has since become a successful commercial enterprise. It doesn't stop there. These days, Mike has become something of a TV personality with his regular contributions as "roving reporter" on emigratetv.com. Little wonder that the Coles won the hearts of both our judging panel and the viewing public, who voted them "Champion Migrants".

With his first-hand experience, no one is better placed than Mike Cole to offer all-round emigration advice to future New Zealand-bound migrants by way of this highly informative book. He's been there, done it *and* got the t-shirt. (And, knowing Mike, he's no doubt made sure that BritsNZ is screen-printed all over it!)

Colin Marchant
Founder and programme director, EmigrateTV.com
December 2008

Mike, Alex and family,
I am so thrilled you decided to join us in New Plymouth, New Zealand!

Since the first time we met at an Emigrate Show in England, it's been a pretty exciting roller coaster ride for you all. And the great thing is you've brought others along for the ride. Every time another family decides to relocate, this community is the better for it.

Recently New Plymouth has been judged the best place to live in New Zealand, and only last month the best place to live in the world. The contribution of our new settlers has been a big part of that recognition.

As Mayor, I am often privileged to meet folk who are looking at relocating from other parts of the world; to welcome new residents to this community; and in many cases to conduct citizenship ceremonies for those very same people.

It's just such an honour I've had with your family. You have become our roving ambassadors, and by encouraging and supporting others in making the move to join us in this community (with books such as this one), I think lives have been enriched, and this community has been enhanced by your efforts.

On behalf of this community, I thank you all.
Keep the passion!

Peter Tennent
New Plymouth Mayor
December 2008

CONTENTS

PART 1

INTRODUCTION

G'day and Haere Mai (Maori for "WELCOME")

Thank you very much for choosing to read our book.

This is a story of how the Cole family (that would be us then!) totally changed their lives by opting to pick themselves up, leave the UK and start a new life in New Zealand.

Whilst it is very much New Zealand focused, this story is relevant to anyone looking to emigrate, no matter to which country – the tips and advice and stories are common across most migrants and we trust you will gain something useful from this book.

This is not a nuts and bolts explanation of what you need to do to emigrate – that will be for our future books which are already virtually written – but rather a story of an ordinary family who went and did something extraordinary, just like all other migrants and just like you will do if your dream is to leave the UK and migrate to a new life in a new country!

However, this is a story of more than just our migration from the UK – it's about an awakening, of a realisation that in reality we can, as people, do whatever we want to do with focus and determination, self-belief and passion. Many of these virtues are fundamental to the British way of life (how else could we have built an empire?), but are too often trampled underfoot these days by the apparent need to run to keep up (with what and for whom, of course, no-one can readily say) and because we have become attuned to remaining in our places – the good old class system at its worst!

We learnt from this move that all things are possible and that it is usually others who put your doubts in place. With a tad of courage, a whole lot of conviction and focus anything is possible! Of course there will be tough times, rough times and sacrifices to be made but if you are determined enough these simply become challenges which you can overcome!

Our hope is that this book inspires you.

Interestingly, we have often remarked that we have no idea what the spark was that allowed us to see our future so clearly or quite where the determination came from, or where the passion to move came from, or quite how we changed our lives so dramatically. In 2007 we came into contact with a DVD and book called The Secret (www.thesecret.tv) which is about the power we all hold in us, particularly when we act positively and "ask" the universe for help in our endeavours. As part of your process for looking at migrating, moving or simply changing, you could do a lot worse than watching the DVD or reading the book!

In conclusion we trust you enjoy reading our story and that it inspires you to reach for your dreams – with focus and determination they are attainable!

Early advice:

- Move 110% - "cut the ties" and "burn the bridges" and leave the UK as if you are never coming back.

- Migrating (or simply moving house) is as much a mental thing as a physical thing – get your head right and everything else will follow!

- Do everything with passion – listen to your gut and put your heart and soul into the process.

- See things as challenges and not problems – to me a problem has a negative vibe about it whilst a challenge is something positive – you rise to it and actively seek a way over, under, around or through a challenge!

- Parents – stop worrying about your kids (no matter what their ages). They will adopt and adapt a whole lot more easily than you will – trust me; we see it all the time!

"You can do anything if you have enthusiasm." - **Henry Ford**

"We cannot discover new oceans (and countries) unless we have the courage to lose sight of the shore."

"Enjoy your achievements as well as your plans."

And so the story begins...

Magazine shoot for Australia/New Zealand Magazine – the family on Back Beach, New Plymouth mid-winter (August!) 2006

CAST OF CHARACTERS

Mike

According to my OLDER sisters, I was born just after the dawn of time, but in reality in 1956 in Buckinghamshire. I have two sisters (both older, not that I'm stressing this too much...) but both my parents have now passed on.

I was fortunate as a child to travel widely. My father owned his own businesses at that time and as a kid I would holiday in Europe and the UK and would be taken skiing each year; a fantastic childhood on looking back, within a great family environment where I used to sit and watch Mum and my sisters bake on a Sunday afternoon, where Dad cooked the most awesome meals on a Saturday. I would be taken "down the pub" with Dad on a Sunday for a Coke and crisps!

Christmas was always special, with Dad trying to stuff the turkey which, looking back, was amazing – he seemed able to bring the dead bird to life ... well, at least it seemed to fly around the kitchen with Dad in hot pursuit with the bowl of stuffing in his hand – some might say he'd had a touch too much beer and scotch but I'm not so sure!

Mum was a fantastic cook, too, and just a complete laugh, very much the life and soul, and the bond between her and me was particularly strong. Looking back, though, that is fair to say of the family as a whole. There was always much laughter and fun and adventures to be had.

I was sent away to boarding school – my (older) sisters would claim it was because I was sooooo bad, but Dad had an "old fashioned" view of the way of things and believed that his son should take the opportunity that he and Mum worked so hard to provide – we were definitely not rich, rich but mum and dad worked hard and created a lifestyle and opted to privately educate me. Without doubt, this was to mould my future by creating my ability to act independently and allowing me to build life-long friendships – but - trust me - I hated having to go back to school and leave my family ALL the way through my school life – it was never a happy experience for me!

While I excelled at sport, in particular – rugby, unfortunately, this did not easily translate into the classroom (and if my kids are reading this, take note – study hard!) although I managed to get seven or eight "O" levels and one "A" level whilst at school. (I subsequently got a further "A" level at night school – an awakening that perhaps I should have studied a bit harder at school!)

I played representative rugby at County level and enjoyed all sports, willing to try most everything.

I never quite knew what I wanted, work-wise, and I suppose envied those who seemed to clearly know what they wanted to do. I also lived, for far too long, under the impression that others were better and more knowledgeable than me: it would only be when we started this journey to New Zealand that the self-realisation came that I was a more-than-capable person who could do whatever he put his mind and soul to.

I worked in the life assurance and investment industry for all my time in the UK, initially for the Equitable Life Assurance Society in Aylesbury, Bucks within various admin and underwriting teams both as a "worker" and a manager, and then as a Financial Adviser with them in Chelmsford, Essex. Like far too many excellent clients, I suffered the fate of senior managers, in their total arrogance, managing to ruin a fantastic company for whom I worked – the end came with a House of Lords ruling that effectively closed the company. The next day my youngest child, Gabriella, was born and whilst Alex was doing an amazing job of bringing her into the world I don't think I was helping by pushing back and commenting that the timing was wrong as Daddy might no longer have a job!

Whilst Equitable stayed together for a while longer and then moved into the Halifax stable, too much had changed too much and it became apparent I needed to move on and so I joined Scottish Widows as a Financial Adviser and cannot speak highly enough of them as a company, employer or group of colleagues – they were simply outstanding!

There were some great times with Equitable Life and I worked with some magic people, moving up the organisation, but, as usual, there were also some bad times, times when the rebel inside me reared up. This usually occurred when being required to do things by people who failed to engender respect and who simply could not manage the proverbial p*** up in a brewery...

Sanity, work-wise, came with the opportunity to go out into the field and become a front-line Financial Adviser. I felt that I had finally found a place in life where I fitted. Perhaps this was because I was working within a much looser structure; being in a company but having some independence.

I met Alex when least expecting to do so and was instantly beguiled by her. She was a little coy initially but soon warmed to me – must have been when I offered to take her on holiday!

I married her over nineteen years ago (so will be up for parole soon!) and we have three great kids. Our life together has been a roller-coaster at times but we have always known we were a great fit and, without doubt, this move to New Zealand could not have happened without Alex embracing the whole thing one hundred percent. Indeed, she was the instigator of the move and was the rock that allowed all this to happen.

She can be stubborn and our outlook on life and people is different, although very much complementary, and in many ways she has made a remarkable transformation since leaving the UK – I am extremely proud of her as a woman, wife and mother.

I also have a "previous" wife, Julie, who now lives in Northern France and who is God-mother to Jacob and Gabriella, but she and I did not have children. She has always been interested in and encouraging of our plans.

Looking back, I think that a good deal of my life experience was aimed at getting me to New Zealand – I know, I know it sounds weird, but by being reflective that really is how I feel! My schooling taught me the ideals of independent thinking and working in large companies gave me the tools I needed, from true customer service to management principles to identifying that actually my best boss would be myself (and I have my wife's permission to say that!). Whilst, initially, coming to New Zealand meant working for someone else, the long-term aim had always been to work for myself.

I don't think we could ever have envisaged how that would all come about, nor what we would go through to get to that "Independence Day"...

Alex

A complex character rather like a fine wine, Alex was born in the swinging '60s (and boy did she grab all the rhythm going!) and with an English mum and Greek Dad she was blessed with skin that tanned at the first hint of sun without burning – that seems to have disappeared a little with the birth of the kids – the price she has paid for motherhood!

Alex had a step-brother, Billy, and a sister, Gina. Bill sadly died just six months into our time in New Zealand and, whilst we had known before we left that he was unwell, it was still a huge shock which immediately and graphically illustrated just how far away we really were – intellectually we knew this but the reality is always that bit different.

Alex was born, educated and bought up in Berkhamsted, Hertfordshire and, rather like me, did not excel at school...but did excel at running a household and looking after her family, and dancing. In fact, she was occasionally allowed to skive school. (Don't look kids - that was very naughty and Grandma was naughty for allowing her to do so.)

She did, however, excel at dance...and was both a cheer-leader and a member of a dance group, where she made friends who endure to this day. She has a totally natural rhythm (unlike me, who doesn't even have two left feet!) and can pick up the beat really easily. This was a key factor in her becoming a keep fit and aerobics instructor after Joe was born and, whilst she did not have the same confidence in her own abilities then as she does now, she did an amazing job and was an excellent teacher/instructor.

She had a totally different childhood to mine, but managed to spend fun times with cousins during the summer holidays and would disappear off to Greece occasionally, usually in the back of a car! Life, however, was tough at times and there was a period when her dad went back to Greece to work simply to build extra funds for the family. At these times she had to learn to run the house and help her mum keep things neat and tidy – a trait that carries on today, much to the disgust of our kids!

There were times when she thought about being a hairdresser, or, rather, there was a time when she cut her sister's hair for her, which was, perhaps, an early realisation that maybe she didn't have the scissor skills required. I can't fathom whether her sister has a wonky head or whether her hair has just never grown out straight again!

At the earliest opportunity Alex looked to leave school and transferred from being a Saturday girl in a local travel agent to working full-time, simply happy to go to work.

She worked in travel in Berkhamsted, Harrow and Aylesbury before we met, and then, after the kids, in Buckingham. She moved from the small independent agency in Berkhamsted to Hogg Robinson in Hemel and then moved to Harrow when she started managing the shop. She then moved to Aylesbury and it was here that fate intervened and we met, when I was booking a holiday. Suffice to say she threw herself at me (which girl wouldn't?) and I quickly recognised the possibility of great travel and cheap holidays. Oh, and I also found her totally captivating!

She managed to embrace a life with differences – she loved the fact that I'm the cook and that I would always have something rustled up for her. She magnificently managed to grit her teeth and give up part of her day off mid-week to be taken for walks by my dad – mind it always ended at a pub lunch so there were compensations...but this from a girl who had to have her feet actually put on the floor each morning to actually get her moving out of her pit and off to work!

Alex is terrific when it comes to being a mum and, when carrying Joe, was great at simply going with the flow and resting when her body told her to do so –

even the realisation that this would not be as easy with numbers two and three never diminished her desire or joy in being a mum!

Unfortunately, some two months after Joe was born, my father died, which somewhat overwhelmed us and masked the fact that Alex was having some post-natal depression problems. We eventually realised this might be the case but it was a tough time for her and she coped brilliantly.

Similarly, when Jacob was born, a month previously she had me in hospital for a serious operation, my job completely shot to pieces by a company re-shuffle and me applying for another job. We then had Joe in hospital having grommets put in his ears to help his hearing. Not exactly a relaxing schedule for a heavily pregnant mum...

Again things were not exactly great when Gabriella was due. By that time, whilst my job was running smoothly and we were all enjoying life in Essex, the Equitable Life's existence was almost at an end. Indeed, the day that Gabriella started her journey into the world the House of Lords decided that the end was not nigh but actually here. There was Alex desperately wanting to push and I was asking her to hold on until I knew whether I still had a job but we were already attuned to "going with the flow" and so Gabriella arrived, albeit with a huge scare. Alex had done all the hard work without any drugs and simply with great focus and determination and then we almost lost her at birth but the staff at Chelmsford hospital were simply amazing. Working in dilapidated buildings and under trying conditions, they performed brilliantly and we had the little girl that Alex had so badly wanted. Amazingly, and with no particular foresight, we had managed to have our three terrors almost exactly five years apart each time.

Looking back I should not have been surprised at how well organised we all were when we left the UK as Alex is just that sort of girl – she was always well organised at the birth of the kids and had managed our move from Buckingham to north Essex. Moving to New Zealand, no problem mate!

Joe

Born in 1990, he was a surprise, because although we had called the baby Joe all the way through the pregnancy we had, for some reason, always expected a girl. At least when he arrived he had a ready-made name!

He was of course "special" in that he carried on the family name and I don't think there was anyone more proud than my dad to hear the news; it was great to see him and Alex's mum and dad at the hospital visiting the new arrival. Whilst he was not Dad's first grandchild, he was Alex's parents' and it was a joyful time. It was, therefore, with added sadness that we lost Dad so soon after Joe arrived – but as he occasionally reminds his brother and sister, he was held and cuddled by Grandad Cole!

Joe became a well-travelled little chap, visiting Europe, the Caribbean and the USA before his little bro turned up.

Alex used to worry that he was not keeping up with others and I am sure other parents go through these agonies. I always felt, though, that whilst he could not count as high or read as many words as others, he had fantastic motor skills and was very adept at all things sporting. It is now clear that he is like his parents in not being the most academic kid on the block and whilst he has passed all his NCEA levels so far (the equivalent to GCSEs in the UK) and is still at school, there is always a nagging feeling that he could do better with a little more application...just like his father!

He is still, however, a very accomplished sportsman, being very good at football (albeit that, frustratingly, he lacks that edge of self-confidence to move to the next step which he certainly has the ability to achieve). He has also taken to surfing, snowboarding and, in particular, skateboarding.

He had a really good group of mates in the UK, with whom he went all the way through primary school and on into high school and, whilst he was really positive about the move to New Zealand, that changed when sitting at Heathrow awaiting the plane's departure and speaking with his mates on the mobile during their break time. At that point, his attitude changed and he became a nightmare. It took some three-and-a-half years to get over it and to really settle in New Zealand.

TIP: *Leave the day before – say your goodbyes and take yourselves off to a hotel near your departure airport and have some family time before flying out – this effectively help reduce the emotional stress of leaving!*

When you leave home for that final time, gather all the mobile phones together, switch them off and do not turn them on again until you are in New Zealand: your kids talking to friends on the mobile when leaving is just like having that friend sitting next to them at the departure gate – it's just too hard and you do not need an increased emotional state when you have so far to travel.

Of course, being his parents, we were the last to realise that he was also going through puberty, and as we noticed on our first trip back to the UK after eighteen months away, he was way ahead of most of his peers which, of course, didn't help any. He *did* turn into the grunting, monosyllabic teenager so wonderfully portrayed by Harry Enfield and "Mrs Paterson" and he made life very hard for us. There were times when it was clearly a deliberate act and others when you could see him fighting the hormones raging through him.

For us it was very important that we allowed him to do all the things that Kiwi-born-and-bred kids could do at any given age, so we allowed him to start driving when he hit his fifteenth birthday. No, that's not a misprint; here in New Zealand, the kids can start driving at age fifteen. He has done remarkably well through the process and got his full licence before he was seventeen - something obviously not possible in the UK. That sense of freedom made a huge change in his lifestyle, even if he thought it didn't: it took a while for him to grasp and appreciate that, at sixteen, he could legally walk out of the house, jump into his car and just go, whether it was round to his mate, off to school, off surfing or up the mountain to snowboard. All of that would have been impossible in the UK.

To his credit, he has weathered the storms and is now really well settled and adjusted and looking to his future.

We now need to sit down and identify what he wants to do next, as he leaves school in November. He has indicated an interest in plumbing, in working for the Customs Service or being a policeman. We feel he would be better suited to the plumbing role, as we feel he will want to be his own boss one day, which would be possible as a plumber, and it would also give him the ability to travel and work. But...watch this space!

Jacob

Jake arrived in our lives when we were at a low ebb because of job and health issues and he was just such a happy little chappy from the get go! He was born in 1995 just after Joe started school, which allowed Alex to spend a good deal of time with him during the day and not have too much jealousy from Joe.

Of course, being number two, he was always following in his brother's footsteps, but as he got older it was interesting to see how his do-anything attitude often made Joe do things that perhaps he'd not normally do. For instance, Jake has little fear and so fairground rides are just a hoot for him and, for Joe, if Jake can and will do it, then he has to do it, too.

Jake has a real affinity with animals - simply loves them to pieces - and we would expect to see him to do something with animals for a living. He has already run a dog walking service here in New Zealand - quite the little entrepreneur!

He was always a really cruisey kid and very adaptable, simply going with the flow. Whilst not overtly sporting, he is more than capable and is more of a rugby player than a footballer. He has a completely natural ability in distance/cross-country running. He is now starting to skateboard and we are amazed at how readily he has progressed as a snowboarder.

School for Jake, whilst not exactly being a breeze, is pretty straightforward. He is definitely capable and, with a little application, will do well, but key for him is the interaction with the teacher and if he likes them he does well.

Jake was just eight when we left the UK and he was probably at a great age to do so; intellectually not really aware of exactly what was happening but capable of helping and enjoying the experience. It was not until we were halfway to LA on the flight to New Zealand that we realised that Jake had not quite grasped the distance we were going – he asked if one of his friends could come and stay for the weekend! I'm not sure how we could have made that more real for him but I think he had grasped what was happening by the end of the flight(s).

Jake probably adapted the quickest to the new life in New Zealand – shoes were off really quickly, and stayed off, and he definitely adapted his ideas and views to those of a Kiwi kid. He has a Kiwi accent, which he told me the other day boys seem to hear, whereas the girls seem quite able to tell he's British. I have told him that if he simply spoke to them instead of kissing them with his English lips, they'd not spot the English in him so easily – for some reason I now have a big bruise on my arm!

Jake has managed to give us the biggest health scare here in New Zealand.

He became really poorly with a nasty rash and the doctors thought that he had meningitis. They whisked him straight into hospital and ran a battery of tests and he and I spent a night there whilst they at least cleared him of meningitis.

It appeared that he probably had an allergic reaction to horses, which was a blow: before we left, we got the boys to tell us what they wanted to do in New Zealand that they either did not or could not do in the UK. Joe wanted to surf and Jake wanted to ride horses.

We were very focused on getting the kids to look forward as much as possible and have something to achieve once in New Zealand and we made sure both got their wish pretty soon after arriving. So, Jake started riding and had this brief brush with allergy, which has not returned so it might just have been that particular horse!

Surprisingly we have found it hard to find riding schools here in New Plymouth and each time we have they have ended up closing, but Jake has learnt well and is quite competent but perhaps not enough so for us to look at a horse purchase!

TIP: *To get the kids looking forward positively, if old enough (say seven+), get them to identify something that they can do in their new country that they do not/cannot do in the UK – make sure it happens soon after arrival!*

Gabriella

Ah, the baby of the family! But, of course, being the youngest AND a girl, she is very much the ruler of the family. And smart too!

Born in 2000 and having survived that early scare at birth, she subsequently spent a week under the infrared lamps trying to control jaundice – obviously not ready to go home at all!

She was an absolute delight and we felt very lucky that we had a third perfect and healthy child – I had genuinely believed we were "pushing the envelope" a third time so we were both relieved once Gabs was declared fit enough to come home!

She soon realised, however, that she had four people who would do anything to make her stop screaming and so effectively chose not to speak for nigh on three years. When she eventually did so, it was pretty much in her own language, which thankfully Jakey always seemed to understand.

Added to that, she did not sleep a whole night through for over three years – the only saving grace to that being that she was a happy child during the day and not a misery. (Her *parents* were on their knees, but *she* was happy!) We always knew she could understand us and that, as a family, we did not help ourselves by "pandering" to her but c'est la vie.

At just over three years old when we left, Gabriella was at an age where she had no concept of what was happening, although she seemed to understand that she'd not see her grandparents for a while. For her, though, it was really just another day and she took things very much in her stride. Suffice to say, she has now spent more of her life in New Zealand than in the UK and we are struggling to understand where all that time has gone.

She adapted in a more natural way to life in New Zealand and is very much the Kiwi kid in her whole outlook to life – doesn't wear shoes, speaks with an accent and is generally positive about life.

She has entered school, having been through kindergarten, (nursery) and has therefore been through the whole system in New Zealand and, in our opinion, is being better served by this system than the boys were in the UK.

She appears to take everything in her stride and is showing signs of being quite capable at school, but as for sport, we are not sure yet. She is quite a fast runner, though, so we will see what happens.

Helpful Hobbits

John & Daphne Fry

These lovely people, Welsh to the core, and friends from way back, were the first to help us on the road to New Zealand. When we went to see an Emigration Agent, who was based in Chester, John and Daph, who lived in North Wales, immediately offered a bed and childcare, thus allowing Alex and me to make the meeting. They then sat and listened and questioned what had happened and what everything meant – again invaluable at that early stage.

Thank you guys – you very much allowed us to get the ball rolling!

Karen & Peter Goadby

With friends like these you know you must have done something right in a former life.

Always there with penetrating questions, sage words and ideas to test our resolve, perhaps the most annoying thing is that they would never let us get away with a "brush off" answer, which, of course, was invaluable.

They have always been there for us and it is an absolute delight to go and spend a couple of nights with them when I am back in the UK. They are always interested and the penetrating questions still come thick and fast but as they too are in business it is always good to bounce things off them.

They were excellent with the kids and to see Joe open up with them last year in Cornwall and talk about a whole range of things was amazing. Rest assured, as a hormonally challenged teenager he's back to grunting! They were similarly great with little Jake and our then baby girl Gabs!

They know the stresses and strains we went through as they were there for a good deal of it – indeed it was Karen we called in the middle of our cold, first night in New Zealand to see if she could get some action on our three missing bags.

Karen, Peter, your friendship has been and is worth far more than mere words can explain and we feel truly honoured and grateful that you have been and remain in our lives – thank you!

Mum & Dad

My mum and dad had both died some time previous to our decision to move to New Zealand, but Alex and I were both convinced that they would have encouraged us to push for our dreams and were with us in spirit!

Alex's mum and dad were never going to be delirious about our moving and taking the grandchildren away but initially were very supportive.

To the normal mix of emotions we had to add the fact that Alex's father is Greek, and so we had an additional "cultural" view on things. To a large degree, the Greek way is that the eldest daughter (that would be Alex!) looks after the parents and even though Alex's mum is English we felt that her father still held sway with this idea.

So, initially, all was good, but once visas were issued and it was a racing certainty that we were, indeed, off to New Zealand, the tables did turn quite markedly and it felt that some serious emotional blackmail was brought to bear.

This was an incredibly difficult time and brought added tensions to an already fraught period and brought unwelcome pressure on our plans to emigrate and on our marriage...leaving Mum and Dad is not easy and of course it is hard on the parents to see their kids and grandchildren up and leg it to the other side of the world! I believe we are extremely fortunate that we recognised this and that Alex had the amazing strength of character to make it through this trying time.

In truth, the whole issue did necessitate a conversation along the lines of them either having the pleasure of seeing Alex and the children right up to departure day or not seeing any of us before we left.

To their immense credit they took on board our comments, recognised what they had been doing and totally changed their outlook toward our plans. They were just the best before we left, helping wherever they could and being fantastic with the kids. What had been a very, very difficult period resolved itself into something really great.

Unfortunately, Alex's dad declared that he would never come to New Zealand and, whilst her mum has been, her dad has not. But (and as I write this in mid-2008, the kids do not know this yet) later in 2008 he will come and stay and even if it is only for a week, Alex will just be so totally overjoyed that he has come and seen what we have created here in New Zealand. The kids will be totally blown away, as they love their Papoo (Greek for Grandfather) to bits, probably because he is a great source of lollies!

Mum and Dad – you are tremendously loved and your support has been invaluable. Even though we have had some very difficult times, we want you to know that you have always been in our hearts and minds – thank you for everything!

Les & Jake

These two are - and no, I cannot resist it - my OLDER sisters.

Each, in her own way, has just been just the best and they have always offered unquestioning support, even if they feared we'd lost our marbles at times.

Les lives in Australia and the fact that she has made the move twice and now lives with such passion for Australia was indeed a great lesson for us: focus on what you want and go with as open a mind as possible, with a willingness to go out and meet people and not sit back and expect people to come to you.

She obviously has the misguided belief that Australia is the best place on earth but we all know the truth - New Zealand is!

She has made the trip to see us twice and, in the face of great adversity, has been so strong and always ready to despatch advice (even, sometimes, when *asked* for...well, she is the eldest AND a teacher!) but is also there to just listen.

Les, I am just so proud of you!

Jake has always been the rock-steady one. Les and I go off doing weird and wonderful spontaneous things and Jake simply appears to cruise through life making things look easy, when, of course, she and her husband have worked incredibly hard to achieve their goals. It was immensely reassuring to always know she was there in the background to turn to if needed and simply having her there was a huge help throughout the move and, indeed, now.

Jake, I am so proud of all that you and John have achieved (so now really grasp and enjoy your retirement – you have earned the time together, so enjoy) and for having you as my sister I feel great fortune – thank you!

Lindsay & Gus

With friends like these you could ask why we ended up so lucky - again!

During our journey down the emigration road, they were with us every step of the way, simply coming in the back door and helping us clear the wine cellar so selflessly. I had told Alex to not mention the fact that we couldn't take it with us, but again their selfless devotion to helping us to dispose of that wine – well medals are simply not enough!

They were with us when we first sat in Thetford Forest hatching the idea of moving and were always supportive and encouraging. Their friendship means a huge amount to us and it continues today, as they always provide a place for me to stay when I'm over in the UK for the emigration shows. OK, I have to cook and clean but that's a small price to pay...

Thank you, guys, for all your help, encouragement and simply for being just the best friends!

Richard & Rosie

From being "just" a couple we lived near and to whom we chatted as we walked the kids to/from school, they became great friends who could always be relied on to lift our flagging spirits. They were always interested in what was happening and could always get us to see the positives – thanks guys!

Mandy Mitten

Mandy was our Visa Agent and is getting a mention not because she helped get our visas - after all, that is what we paid the company to do - but once it became clear that the initial advice we had been given and the papers we had submitted for our Long Term Business Visa were not accurate, she went the extra mile. She let us know that she had seen someone with my UK qualifications get the "right" grading for visa purposes from the New Zealand Qualifications Authority. But for those actions, we could still be trying to get into New Zealand.

She identified what needed to be done, guided us through the stages and then checked our application prior to our submission to New Zealand Immigration. Without that input at that time, we would not be here now. If you like, the actions she took were the perfect demonstration of excellent customer service!

Bruce Burrows

Bruce worked for Immigration in London and I am not sure to this day how we actually found him, but he, again, was excellent.

When we had our Long-Term Business Visa bounced, he stepped in and reviewed the papers and file, even though it was not actually in his remit to do so, and advised us what action to take to try and get a positive appeal. When we then found the way into New Zealand through my UK qualifications and permanent residency, he organised for us to talk to the right people in London, had our medicals extended and was probably instrumental in making residency happen by getting our case seen by the right people quickly.

Again, excellence in customer service!

Markham Lee

Markham acted as our New Zealand solicitor when we were looking at buying a business. (This was when we started out trying to come into New Zealand via the Long-Term Business Visa route.)

He helped with many aspects of that application, from pulling a business plan together, to helping with the due diligence, to being a sounding board for the offer price, and he came into his own when we needed to launch an appeal against being turned down for said visa.

It was at this point that we found we theoretically needed to be in New Zealand to be allowed to appeal against the decision and he managed, even though in Thailand at the time, to organise events and contacts so that we could make a formal appeal and additional submissions.

I had met Markham on my fact-finding trip to New Zealand and, apart from his blinkered view that New Zealand were the best at rugby and cricket (what??), he was a thoroughly nice guy who again gave above and beyond.

He has our heartfelt thanks that he made one of our initial contacts with a Kiwi so positive!

Scottish Widows & My Colleagues

Fortunately, for a good period during our time trying to get to New Zealand, business was quiet, which enabled me to do all the things I needed to do for our move, whilst still keeping the "day" job going.

Like most people, I really did not need/want them to know my plans too early, just in case, but as soon as I told everyone they could not have been more understanding and helpful. They allowed me to pretty much do what I wanted, but would not put my resignation into effect until the day we left for New Zealand, thereby allowing me to keep my company car. All they required was for me to answer the phone and to see people, if that was needed, and I was more than happy to do so. Their support was invaluable and we were very grateful to them for that.

Robert & Gill

I spent a good number of years working with Robert and it is strange how you can do that before a chance conversation suddenly reveals that you have friends in common and have probably met before in your teenage years. That happened with Robert and Gill. We discovered mutual friends and then came the realisation that we must have partied together at some stage – weird but true.

There followed another chance conversation about moving to New Zealand and – lo and behold – we discovered that Robert and Gill used to live here and were, therefore, able to give some really insightful and helpful information.

Rob and Gill – thanks so much for your friendship and invaluable input. It was always so welcome and usually very timely!

Colin Marchant

What can we say about this chap? There's probably a lot he would wish me not to say, but the role he played in our move and settlement in New Zealand can never be underestimated.

Colin used to be the MD of Outbound Publishing and we regularly got their newspaper, Emigrate New

Zealand. It was in an edition of this paper that I saw advertised a request for a family to keep a video diary of their move to New Zealand.

Colin had been responsible for an earlier DVD diary of migrant families moving to various locations and we had watched that with great interest. He had been let down on his second such DVD and needed someone urgently. Being in need of an excuse to buy a new video camera, I applied for the Coles to be the New Zealand-bound family. Alex never quite believed that I had actually applied until Colin rang and asked us to send a demo tape.

To me, this was a perfect way to focus on what we needed to do and to build a family record of our move. The fact that we were led only slightly awry was neither here nor there: we took the challenge of being the New Zealand-bound family on his new DVD, *The Migrant Challenge,* and proceeded to film our highs and lows, laughter and tears. It was huge fun and Colin and his wonderful wife, Caroline (affectionately known as Lady M), were simply awesome.

Colin was instrumental in getting us back into the UK after eighteen months to sit in front of audiences and talk about our experiences and, in no small part, in actually giving us the tools and confidence to create our own company, BritsNZ.

That first time back was such a revelation to us – people were actually interested in what we had to say and, whilst for Alex it was incredibly scary, I felt very much at home with an audience and just revelled in it, even though Colin managed to reduce me to tears at one seminar: not by being 'orrible, but by creating a DVD that made me revisit our emotions in such a raw way that I was straight back there as though it were happening all over again.

Without any doubt, our experiences with the filming opened a huge number of doors for us. Sure, we ourselves very much made that happen but, in his own way, Colin was a driver. From that single advert has come a fantastic history store for our family, our company, appearances on national radio and TV here in New Zealand and further appearances at emigrate shows.

Colin and Lady M, your kindness, humour and courtesy to both Alex and me was, and is, simply amazing and our thanks are both heartfelt and unlimited!

PART 2

WHERE DID WE START?

For us, it probably began on a campsite in Thetford Forest, at the Dower House. The kids were roaming freely and safely without a care in the world. Alex and I were able to sit out in the warm evening sunshine (yes, they did still have warm evenings in the UK in 2002/03), relaxing and thinking, "Why not more of this?" We talked about what the UK stood for at that time; what would the future be in that country for our children, who were eleven, six and two at the time? What was our future in relation to work, taxes and the government? How safe did we really feel?

We concluded that we were dissatisfied with a number of things: we were working harder; it seemed, only to go backwards. We were concerned about our children's future, which didn't look awfully bright, and about their safety (as well as our own) in a country which was becoming more dangerous by the day, in terms of both terrorism and simple day-to-day living. Our home at the time was on a new development in Essex and already the drugs culture was rearing its insidious and terrifying head. Perhaps just as terrifying was the fact that our eldest son (aged 10 at the time) understood it all, having had the police at his school to talk about drugs in general. I can well remember that the only talk we had at school was the excruciatingly horrible "sex talk"!

I had always been keen to travel and to work and live offshore and now we began to seriously look at the process.

Our initial concerns were, of course, where to go and how we would all deal with leaving family behind. My parents had both passed away, but I had a sister in the UK and one in Australia. Alex had both parents and siblings in the UK. Leaving was never going to be the easy option, but, nevertheless, we decided the time had come to get out of our rut and to face some new fears and challenges.

We spent a glorious two weeks in Portugal, (staying in the place now made infamous by the sad case of Madeline McCann) thinking, while away from everyday stresses, about the whole concept, about our destination and how the kids would cope. Since we were now quite certain that a move abroad was the right thing for us, we managed to put to the backs of our minds the concerns about our relatives' reactions and to concentrate on geography.

Naturally, our first ideas centred on Europe, because of its proximity to Britain and because we had known parts of it after holidaying there. There was, however, the obvious language barrier as witnessed when watching TV programmes following poor English folk trying to build a new life in their favourite holiday destination: while they may have thought through the process quite carefully, never did it seem to cross their minds that they may have to learn the lingo!

Following this thread we then considered the other English-speaking countries. Canada, while beautiful, is undoubtedly cold for large parts of the year and with Alex half-full of Greek blood, cold is not good – so scratch Canada. However a big plus for Canada is again its proximity to the UK but this was not sufficient to outweigh the cold!

The USA was attractive, because it offered an opportunity to work for ourselves, but the issues surrounding crime and the gun culture and the obvious difficulties of obtaining a semblance of a permanent visa were sufficient to put us off. Scratch the USA!

The Caribbean is warm, certainly, and beautiful, and whilst we understood and very much liked the educational system, we were very concerned that it would be too small and insular – scratch the Caribbean!

Australia seemed a good bet, therefore, particularly with my sister and a friend of Alex's already there to help smooth the path. The main concerns, however, were the potentially lethal insects, snakes and other hazards. I know there are plenty of Aussies out there who shake their heads at this notion and find it all a little bit wimpish but the reality for us would have been the lack of "street wisdom" of our kids – and given that my sister has found a rather large snake in her urban garden this is not just a "bush" thing and we were not prepared to put our kids in this potentially dangerous situation. We also felt that the temperature was either hot, hot or hotter and saw little point in going to a country where the temperature may be an influence on whether the kids could play outside. Scratch Australia!

So it was that we came to consider New Zealand.

Along with the shared language, there were similarities between New Zealand and the UK, with its green fields and temperate climate (we recognised that we would have missed the changing seasons). The educational systems were also alike and we felt that the kids would be safer from the worries that daunted us in England.

Interestingly, once we started looking at New Zealand, an astonishing number of people popped out of the woodwork who had been there, knew a Kiwi or two or, indeed, and much to our surprise, actually *were* Kiwis!

No one seemed to have a negative word to say about the country or the people and it soon felt like it was pre-ordained that we head there. In fact, one thing that we slowly learned throughout this process was that we needed to heed what was happening around us and listen to what our gut was telling us. That sounds terribly airy-fairy, but I have no doubt now that we were very firmly pushed towards New Zealand by powers unseen!

It seemed, then, that the decision was made, but immediately we discovered that this was only the first and, it soon became plain, the easiest hurdle to get over: New Zealand is a big country (a slightly bigger land mass than the UK, but with only five million people – ahhh, the space!) and it soon became obvious that we needed to narrow down our options to a specific location in which to look at settling.

TIP: *This is a key process for you, as you really do NOT want to spend time, effort (and potentially money) only to realise that you don't really want to go to the country you've been aiming at. Take your time and clearly identify what it is you're looking for and – just as importantly – what you DON'T want, and eliminate those countries that don't fit.*

The Internet really came into its own during this time and we found a great many sites concerning New Zealand, most of which were very helpful. One area we soon recognised we needed to treat carefully, however, were the "forum" style websites. There are a few good ones out there, but most, unfortunately, in our opinion, were simply a place to moan about and somewhat distort the picture of New Zealand... this is NOT to say that the views expressed were not appropriate to that person but there was too often just too much negativity, rather than, here's a problem we have had and this is what we did!

We were fortunate, very early on, to be pointed towards the, as it was then known, *Destination New Zealand* newspaper produced by Outbound Publishing which is now called *Emigrate New Zealand* and their website at www.emigrate2.co.uk, which proved invaluable as a source of information about New Zealand, with articles about, and by, migrants and about relevant websites and internet searches. It also assisted us in locating an emigration agent, who provided us with lots of basic information.

As part of your research, speaking with an emigration agent should provide you with a very clear picture of what you need in order to get into the country of your choice, how long it is likely to take, what you will need to provide and whether you will need a job before you apply. They should be able to detail the exact process and steps and give you an indication of how much it will cost you in relation to their fees and the host country's Government levies and migrant fees. They may also provide you with an idea of a timeline. Simply talking to them at the research stage should not cost you anything nor should it commit you to using their services unless it becomes blindingly obvious that your circumstances warrant their usage but at some point you will need to make the decision whether to have specialist help or whether you will try and get your visa yourself...just remember that to try yourself and fail does not mean that you cannot go back to an Agent and get them to review things for you – it may just cost you more! Bear in mind also that you will still have your UK lives to run, kids will have school and all their normal social things and doing your own visa application needs time, focus and for you to be orderly – if any of those things become a concern then you might do well to opt to use a specialist!

TIP: *The following is what we would consider the "best" process:*
- *Visa Assessment – identify what Visa you can apply for and whether you need a job offer to enable that Visa to be issued.*
- *Telephone consultation with a professional – and importantly like ourselves, with people who have done this before you so you get the understanding and a view on the emotions involved.*
- *Understanding whether you need a job offer and how that is going to happen and what best to do with your CV!*
- *Talk strategy – about getting a job offer and about making the move to New Zealand.*

All of the above should ideally be FREE of charge – once all this has been done then you should know what costs are involved and to whom.

IF YOUR DESTINATION IS NEW ZEALAND THEN WE CAN DO ALL THIS FOR YOU OR POINT YOU TO OTHERS FOR OTHER DESTINATIONS!

They should also be able to give you access to the other providers you will need throughout the process. One crucial contact should be a financial adviser with experience of both UK and the host country's financial system, so you can get really good advice about all the financial aspects of your move. Next to gaining your visa, there is NOTHING more important than sorting your financial migration – it's all well and good being able to have a visa and a job in your new country but if your finances are a mess, then that in itself may stop or severely hamper your ability to settle!

TIP: At this point, we began to realise that we couldn't do without lists.   Information started coming thick and fast and it's difficult to keep so many points in your head.   We used notebooks as a way to keep our thoughts orderly.

This is about the time that people start asking you for money...

 **MONEY, AGENTS AND EMIGRATE FAIRS**

Money

Money is obviously important and you do need a very good handle on how much you have to hand as cash and how much you will have when you liquidate your assets (house, car, unwanted household items and so on). BUT, in my opinion, if you have decided to go, then this is the time when you have to put the blinkers on and not get stressed by the potential costs. I do not believe you can readily emigrate on a budget, as something unexpected always rears its head. You absolutely need a handle on both available funds and costs and you need to look carefully at each phase and process and identify what you can do yourself and what you really do need to pay someone to do for you: if you cannot deal with that, then you are probably not going to make it.

You have to be absolutely focused on getting to your goal and nothing should be allowed to distract you, whether finances (find away around/over/under/ through the challenge) or family (live your life for yourselves and always remember why you have decided you needed to move on – write it down and look at it often.) Be totally and absolutely one-tracked!

Nevertheless, it's scary to see how much of that pot is going to have to be spent on just getting to your destination...but...DON'T BE DAUNTED BY THAT! As I have said emigrating cannot easily be done on a budget and at the time of writing we know that, for a family to emigrate to New Zealand (and you can't go much further away from the UK than to New Zealand) you should be looking at a total cost of £10,000 to £12,000 to get there.

The key is to retain a one-track mind – emigrate or bust! Rest assured that there were times when we had to take some very deep breaths and keep focused as money seemed to fly out of our bank. Whilst we always knew why and where it was going there were times when it was very uncomfortable but we simply knew where we wanted to be and were totally determined to make it happen.

Agents

Agents do charge fees, but their input is invaluable: they are close to the subject and have all the knowledge you'll need. It may be that you know someone who has used a particular agent and can recommend them, but if not, get on the Internet and do some research on the available agents before you call and ask to have a chat to them. Perhaps you could ask if they have some previous clients who would be happy to talk to you about their experiences with that agent.

In addition, most countries, including New Zealand, now require emigration agents to register with a Government body. Those based in New Zealand must register earlier than those offshore (May 2009) and you should be very wary of those not registered. You should always check that the agent you speak to is so registered.

Without doubt there will be many people who feel confident enough to have a go by themselves and indeed Immigration New Zealand actively look to simplify things to allow people to go through the process themselves...BUT, if you do not like form filing, you do not like the rigidity and discipline you will need to complete the process or have a lifestyle that allows you little time to sit and read and gather papers together and apply for various registrations etc or have either a medical or character "problem" then you should recognise that and look to a visa Agent to work for you.

The reality is that without a visa you simply cannot realise your dream – it is as simple as that! In general terms using a visa Agent who will work to get you that MOST important of documents should cost you no more than 25% of your total moving costs – I would suggest that is OUSTANDING VALUE FOR MONEY in the overall scheme of things and worth every penny/cent and that it is this percentage of your overall spend you need to focus on rather than "just" the fees the agent charges!

Of course it is very difficult to know what is a fair fee and the following is only a guideline, as each person's situation will be different, but for a family of four with no medical or character issues moving to New Zealand, you should be looking at no more than £3,000 to £3,500 for an Agent to get you a Visa – certainly that is the range in which our specialists charge clients, at this time!

Emigrate Fairs

As previously mentioned, get in touch with Outbound Publishing (www.emigrate2.co.uk), and ask them to send you their magazine so that you can keep abreast of what's new and also to find out when the emigration shows are on.

In my opinion these are an absolute must and I recommend that you go to at least one, as you will find a bucket load of information freely available and it is somehow reassuring to see that you are not the only "mad" one looking to escape the UK!

Interestingly, I was speaking with a couple in Wellington whom I had met at one of the emigration shows and they admitted that they had actually got very little from the show, apart from the knowledge that their research had been excellent and that fact alone had vindicated coming to the show. However, even they benefited from speaking to a fellow migrant, who is now looking to help others move...oh, that would be me!

The emigration shows are attended by a great many useful people to whom you can talk and get some free (although potentially limited) advice. Remember that the people at the shows are all running businesses and will be looking to ultimately take you on as a client. My advice is to be very reticent about signing on with anyone (and especially about parting with any money) at the show. The emotions and excitement may cloud your judgment and taking some time to think about things away from that buzz may prevent you from making a potentially costly mistake.

The people you speak to at the show(s) should be willing to give you some time and advice, but more important for you going forward will be actually how and when they follow up after the show: how quickly do they come back to you? What do they offer you? Are they saying anything differently to what they said at the show?

My experience of going to, and working at, these shows is that you will meet, in general, very genuine people – those who have been there and done that will be your most valuable contacts, as they will see things from both sides.

The emigrate shows tend to take place in the spring (February, March and April) and in the autumn (September and October). The spring shows tend to be in Edinburgh, Sandown (south-west London) and Belfast, whereas the autumn shows are, at the time of writing, in Stoneleigh (near Coventry) and Aintree. Your best bet is to jump onto the *Emigrate* magazine website: www.emigrate2.co.uk.

There are other organisations running shows (some where the focus is very much purported to be on jobs – whilst the shows are country specific we do not go to the New Zealand shows as we simply do not like the way the organisers do business and they are hideously expensive!) and they tend to be in London, Leeds, Manchester and Edinburgh. Try looking at www.expo-newzealand.com for more information. but...beware of going to a show simply because it says it will get you a job! You need to do your research and identify whether any companies will be there who need your skills base and, of course, you absolutely must have a very clear idea of what visa you will be able to get and you must know when you could be in a position to move. You should get into a position where a job offer is on the table but you can't (won't) move until your UK property is sold – you must be realistic about these timelines and your ability to move, and "do" the shows at the right time for you.

One thing is for sure; you do NOT want to split your family up by having someone in your new country, working, and the other half in the UK with the kids – it is just too stressful and in most cases creates more problems and issues than it solves. And for you ex-armed forces people out there who say that they have done it this way before I have a simple message for you: "No you haven't." Being posted by the British Forces around the world is not the same as you now emigrating – one is a temporary thing with the family fully supported by the system and the other is a life changing permanent move for the whole family with potentially no back up support.

The shows also offer the opportunity to attend seminars where guest speakers will talk to you about all aspects of your move, from visas to what to take with you, to your finances, to changing money, to schooling – you name it and a seminar will be going on which will cover all the issues. If you miss one you wanted to see, find out who was speaking and hunt them down on their stand.

Going to a show should be a must, so definitely add this to your new list of things to do!

We chose an agent based in Chester and we opted to travel to their offices for a meeting to discuss our options and the way forward. Alex will want to tell you that we could have waited for them to come down to London – somewhat nearer home for us – but I was too impatient to wait and wanted to strike while the iron was hot.

We were fortunate to have friends (John and Daphne Fry) based near Chester, who very kindly stepped up to the plate and not only provided a bed but also childminding services!

At the time of our visit, we were still uncertain as to whether we would be able to get into New Zealand, so there were a few nerves on show, but the agents did everything they could to calm us.

That said, one thing which arose from the meeting was that it seemed unlikely that I would be able to qualify for a visa going purely on my UK financial qualifications and experience, which was a bit of a knock-back. The whole purpose of the discussion, however, was to identify just how to get into New Zealand on a permanent basis, so we looked as widely as possible, although suddenly daunted by what lay ahead, and ended up with the proposition that we attempt to either buy a business or set up a new one, thus entering New Zealand using a Long-Term Business Visa (LTBV).

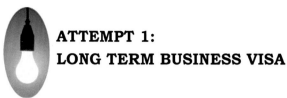

ATTEMPT 1:
LONG TERM BUSINESS VISA

If we had known then what we later found out and know now, perhaps things would have turned out differently, but as we all know, hindsight is a wonderful thing. I think it's fair to say (again, with hindsight) that we didn't fully understand the process or what was going to have to happen to get the visa in place…

The LTBV now requires previous business ownership or senior management experience, but this was not the case back in 2003, or so all parties believed. You must show that this background has provided you with the necessary skills to be involved in your proposed New Zealand business. You can either start a new business or buy into an existing New Zealand business. If you are buying into an existing business, you must take at least twenty-five percent of the shareholding.

A business plan must be prepared and submitted to Immigration. If accepted, you are granted an initial nine months' work visa and you must arrive in New Zealand and have started your business within that period. You will then be granted the balance of the work permit of up to three years. Once you have completed a minimum of two years in the business, you can apply for Residency, providing you can prove that you have met the targets set out in your business plan.

You have a maximum of three years to apply for Residency as an entrepreneur. If your business has not progressed sufficiently, you must either abandon the opportunity or apply for a new LTBV.

As you can see, they don't make things easy (and that applies to most of the visas), but given the mess the UK has got itself into with what appears to be no immigration policy and the EU membership rules, perhaps that's no bad thing!

The business plan you present to Immigration needs to show that there will be a benefit to New Zealand and that benefit needs to fall within one or more of the following parameters:

- Creating new employment opportunities;
- Saving a failed or failing company;
- Improving exports; or
- Expanding on existing business concepts, technologies, services or products.

The simple purchase of all or part of an existing business and adding little to it other than new ownership is, in itself, insufficient. We definitely didn't plan to do just that. This was an opportunity for me to finally break free of the corporate world where too many rules were made by people incompetent at their own jobs and where customer service was given lip-service at best.

Interestingly, LTBVs are not dealt with in the UK: they're all sent down to Wellington. On the face of it, this wouldn't appear to be a problem, but it does mean that it takes time for questions to be asked and answered and it becomes less personal, simply because of the distance involved and your inability to actually see anyone dealing with the processing.

I worked for a life assurance company that believed they were really smart to employ a great many graduates and progress them into management. The problem with that was that they missed the point that being a graduate doesn't necessarily mean you are able to deal with and manage people. The company eventually went to the wall through the arrogance of the senior managers and the Board, who chose not to listen to those who could have provided practical, viable solutions which would, in all probability, not only have saved the company but also headed off the demise of the old faithful With Profit Fund investment. But, to return to the story...

In essence (and slightly bizarrely), we needed to prove to Immigration New Zealand that we could afford to buy and run the business and maintain the family, all without taking a cent in income. Honestly – not the most realistic approach! The temporary nature of the LTBV also means that you cannot have access to any State assistance. This is without doubt the most difficult visa to obtain and gives you the least security for those initial two or three years and even those with business experience in the UK should not assume that they will get a visa in New Zealand. We know of many a case where a visa has been declined, even though the person runs a business in the UK!

Buying a Business

It is truly amazing what you can find on the Net these days and Alex got to work tracking down the types of businesses we thought we'd like to look into. There were loads of different things, from picture framing to campervan hire to florist's etc.

We knew we would like to be in the recreation business and initially looked for a camp site to buy, but at the time the ones we found we thought were too expensive (perhaps not in hindsight). So the alternative we came up with was to look for a camping shop, as this covered the area of interest. We eventually hit upon the concept of a camping and kayak business and started corresponding with two such businesses on the North Island - one in Hamilton and t'other in Whangarei.

At the same time, I was busy looking on the Net for help in sorting out a business plan and found an excellent e-book from the USA which gave a really good picture of the buying process and how to value a business and the different ways in which to finance such an enterprise. The publication was from the Diomo Corporation a.k.a The Business Buyer Resource Centre. The e-book was called "*How to Buy A Good Business at a Great Price*" by Richard Parker (www.diomo.com) who was available to me online once I had purchased and who was extremely helpful and generous with his time – a much needed boost at a critical time.

Whilst we wanted to inject a degree of urgency into the proceedings we were somewhat thwarted with the Whangarei business by the owner being away and with the Hamilton place by an incredibly obstructive Business Broker, who would not supply information requested.

Perseverance paid off in the end and we gathered information about the businesses and their accounts etc. Interestingly, we met with what we thought was a weird problem over confidentiality which we eventually managed to overcome. To us in the UK knowing we couldn't get into New Zealand and not knowing anyone in New Zealand, it seemed odd that the Business Broker was getting so uptight about the whole process. I think we should have been forewarned about this chap at that time; he proved to be a nightmare!

We did as much research as we could on the Net, but it became unavoidable that we needed to go and visit these businesses for ourselves. Here we had a problem in that Alex's mother did not feel she could look after the kids for ten days, so only one of us could go: we felt that the expense of taking the whole family was prohibitive, plus we did not really look at this as a holiday, so having the kids in tow was not going to be appropriate. In November 2002 I came out to New Zealand to see the businesses in Whangarei and Hamilton.

I decided on visiting Hamilton first, as this seemed the more likely shop to purchase on basis of size and location. This meant dealing both with the owners and the Business Broker ("BB" - what a pain in the A he was!)

The owners were really nice, but through all my meetings it was obvious that the BB had not grasped the nature of the business. Also, on walking into the business the first time, (having travelled half way around the world) I was greeted by the owners saying that they were amazed I'd come and surprised that I had shown interest as they had believed that the business had been taken off the market - apparently the BB had forgotten to take it off the Internet – and this was the first I was hearing of this!

Things were not looking good at that point and were further complicated when, after spending a full day with the owners, the BB said on dropping me back to the motel that the price was now higher, although this had not been mentioned in any previous email correspondence or during any of the conversation throughout the day!

I managed to also have a good look around Hamilton and the surrounding area and also to take a kayak trip with the owner down the Waikato River on a sunny warm November evening.

In the middle of the week I took a trip to Auckland to meet Markham Lee, our New Zealand lawyer and Business Planner, to talk through the issues with visas (i.e. what I needed to provide for immigration, what structure they wanted to see, and timelines) and how to structure the deal and to see what the legal paperwork would look like. This was invaluable - and it was good to meet the lawyer and see some of Auckland.

On my return to Hamilton I queried the current valuation with the owners, as I was leaving to head toward Whangarei, north of Auckland, and was reassured that the price was as quoted on the Net.

The journey to Whangarei was a nightmare caused by an accident on the only bit of motorway south of Auckland and the police being incapable of traffic direction. Anyway, I managed to get there eventually, having driven through some outstanding scenery and up and around some truly amazing mountains and around huge logging trucks.

Whangarei is not actually on the coast but has a deep-water harbour area, which is taken over by a plethora of yachts of all descriptions in a very tranquil setting. The town itself is not huge but is well laid out, with housing rising up the hills or running along the river and multitude of bays.

I was very late in meeting the owner of the camp and kayak shop up there but he had hung on and so we at least managed to have a beer or two and a bite to eat, whilst arranging for me to meet up with him at the business next day.

We had decided that on this section of the trip I would stay in a New Zealand home-stay accommodation, which was out in one of the bays heading toward the coast. It was dark on the way out to the home-stay but it was not difficult to see it was in a wonderful setting. The beauty of home-stay is that you get to meet real Kiwis and also others staying with them - I can highly recommend trying this type of accommodation and if you are ever in Whangarei area then you absolutely have to try and get into the Parua Home-stay and Olive Grove in Parua Bay (www.paruahomestay.homestead.com), as the house is beautifully located and your hosts Pat and Peter are delightful.

The next morning was spent with the owner of the business, looking at what he did and how he did it. Tellingly, he commented that if we did not buy he would wind up the business – unfortunately, even to my untrained eye it looked as if he already was doing so. This seemed to me to put an enormous challenge in front of us, because we would have needed to have moved the shop as the location and space were poor. So, I decided almost immediately that unfortunately this would not be for us - unfortunate as I really liked Whangarei and the coast. There was something very calming and spiritual about the place (and having been back since we arrived I am still of the same impression).

So it was back to Hamilton. Amazingly it took me literally only thirty-five minutes to drive from the north end of Auckland, through the centre (right past the Sky Tower) and out to the south end. Try that through London/Birmingham etc. And the Kiwis think they have major traffic problems in Auckland!

Back in Hamilton it was time to look at the first business again and put in a written offer, as Alex and I had decided during one of many phone calls that this seemed to offer the best opportunity. This on the morning of my evening flight from Auckland!

So off I go to talk things through with the owners and to give them my formal offer with an explanation of how the offer was structured and what we would need to do to get a visa and the likely timeline. I left them with it whilst I went to pack and pay for the motel and take a wander around the town. On my return they seemed to be okay with the price and the terms and verbally agreed to the deal. The problem was that the BB arrived as I was about to go and insisted that the price was too low. The owners did reassure me that they would stick to their word and do the deal at the agreed price.

TIP: *If you opt to take a fact-finding trip or come for an interview and only one person can come, make sure to bring the camera and snap away. Also bring a Dictaphone so that you can describe what is in front of you so those back in the UK will get both a visual look at New Zealand and also a commentary – Alex found it really helpful to be able to hear me describing what I was seeing as I drove/walked around.*

On my return to the UK it was all systems go for getting the business plan finalised, to start drawing up contracts and to start the completion of the visa application forms. Unfortunately, during this period the vendors kept calling and emailing, forcing the price up and their solicitor kept messing around with contracts. It got to the point where it seemed we were being pulled further and further over the barrel and felt we had little option other than to threaten to walk away. At one point the vendor decided that they wanted to discuss the issues at 3 a.m. UK time and were curtly told to call back later! In fact, by this time all I felt like saying was that she could shove her business where the sun don't shine – it was incredibly frustrating being pulled and pushed around by people who kept breaking their word, which was so contrary to everyone else I had met in New Zealand!

Ultimately the deal was struck (about six weeks after returning to the UK, having been very firmly led to believe that a deal was done on my leaving). All parties were "happy" (mmm - looking back, I'd say we were Mr & Mrs Desperate!) with the shape and content and, with the formal signing sorted, it was time to put in the last of the paperwork and get the medicals done.

I must admit that it took us a considerable time to actually press the button that would send the contract to New Zealand by fax, as it seemed and of course was such a momentous thing – this was an incredibly stressful time as we knew we were making a massive commitment for all of us and it would mean such a dramatic change to our lives – there was huge hesitation for Alex and me. The kids were extremely positive about the whole thing and that was a great help in the whole process. Ultimately, Joe (who would later come to be "Mr I Hate New Zealand" – teenagers!) simply walked into the office and pressed the send button!

As part of any visa application for New Zealand (unless your stay is going to be less than one year) you are required to have a full independent medical with blood tests and x-rays – except for children under twelve: those aged twelve to sixteen just have chest x-rays. Immigration provide you with a list of doctors to use and you can "shop around" and find someone that best suits your timeline – we also found that not all quoted the same price...and some like cash! The medicals proved difficult to arrange partly because we were trying to keep costs down, because they did seem to vary and partly because they were seemingly so busy.

In the end we found a doctor to do the medicals. Unfortunately they had to be postponed due to a blizzard shutting the M11 from London through Essex and through Cambridge – chaos would be an understatement – which of course made travelling impossible (ah, fond memories!). Thankfully the doctor decided to do extra days in an effort to catch up so we were only delayed for a very short time.

We were also waiting for the police checks to come back. This is a character check to make sure you have not been in real trouble with the law before – it doesn't show your speeding offences but if you have been in court for anything it will show up. And be aware that New Zealand Immigration wants to know EVERYTHING, even if in the UK you would no longer have to mention such an episode. You are NOT dealing with the UK and New Zealand want to know, so there is little point in complaining – you have to play the game by their rules!

So, it was all a bit tense trying to pull all the pieces together, but this we managed to do. Once they were all together we sent the lot off to our Emigration Agent to check all the paperwork. They suggested a number of alterations, most of which seemed to require me to duplicate information, but we complied and eventually all was ready for the courier to take it off to New Zealand.

Strangely, it is difficult to know what is worse; trying to pull all the pieces together, or waiting for confirmation that the paperwork has all arrived safely in New Zealand.

Thankfully, during this whole time work for me had been slow, which had allowed me to put a fair bit of effort into doing paperwork for New Zealand, but by now the market was turning and so I needed to concentrate on my full-time job. Well, it took the mind off waiting for news.

The one major criticism of the New Zealand Immigration Service ("NZIS") and the Business Visa Unit in particular was the almost total absence of information and feedback - customer service must be an alien concept to them and given that you are parting with a fair bit of dosh some level of customer service should exist, but of course we needed to "tread on egg shells" as these people were deciding our future – polite but firm if necessary!

This state of affairs remains to this day and it is an abiding frustration that the country actively seeks people to come and live and work here but cannot set a system where those migrating can actually speak with the people making these life changing decisions. Even when you have been "allocated" a Case Officer you are still not "allowed" to phone and speak with them and you are "requested" to keep e-mail correspondence to a minimum. In my view this is really not an acceptable way to run the show and this is one key area where INZ need to raise their game somewhat!

Just before Easter, having chased them ourselves and having had our New Zealand lawyer raise questions with them as to timing - remember we were locked into dates on the contract for the business - we finally heard back from some chap in Wellington that our application had been declined.

Obviously this was gutting, but I do recall that the reasons given were not based on our business plan, but rather on the fact that we had not owned a business before and they questioned whether we could maintain ourselves on the funds available assuming that we would take **NO** income from the business which was odd as we had proved that in the business plan. It also seemed to take no account of the fact that I have been in management before, that we had undertaken training to do the job we were taking on and that this just happened to be the time in our lives when we could actually make the break and be our own bosses! It was very evident that Immigration wanted to see something that was grey as very black and white, and I suppose what was even more frustrating was that no effort was made to interview us to get an additional feel to our commitment, passion and ability to run this business.

PART 3

WHAT NOW?

We immediately started to search out our New Zealand lawyer, who was on his travels in Asia and, when we finally found him, he started to put together yet more data and information to add to our application and to start the appeals process - both on points of interpretation of the then NZIS policy/law and on the more emotive points in the application.

This again was not straightforward - it transpired that if we had we been sitting in New Zealand then the appeal would have been automatically allowed BUT as we were in the UK they reserved the right to refuse the appeal! This meant a frantic time of building more information whilst also considering whether one of us needed to decamp to New Zealand again!

In any event, we managed to persuade them on the appeal and to pull together a significant amount of further information and comment as to why we felt we could own a business, why at this point in our lives and how we would support ourselves. We worded everything as strongly as possible without being over the top, but having been declined; you tend to loosen up on your 'be nice' attitude. Without a doubt this was further enhanced when it transpired that the chap who had declined us had not been in business himself and had only just moved from Social Welfare - i.e. he had even less business experience than ourselves...thankfully, this approach has now been stopped and the LTBV is at least looked over by New Zealand accountants so that a "professional" view is given/taken on the merits of a business application. With the help of couriers we got the appeal papers to New Zealand just before their deadline.

We were assigned a particular person to conduct the review and we phoned her to check she had all the original papers and all the appeal papers and reminded her of our contractual dates (which were looming) and her commitment to a timeframe - or so we thought.

At about this time I had seen an advert in the Emigrate New Zealand newspaper asking for a family emigrating to New Zealand to compile a video diary of their move for a DVD about families emigrating to various countries in the world.

Thinking this was the perfect excuse to buy a new video camera I suggested we put ourselves forward – Alex, never believing I would, said she was fine with this! Interestingly, at that time on UK TV, we were seeing the start of the shows where people were shown moving abroad and a number of our friends had suggested more than once that we should contact the TV companies and offer ourselves – at that suggestion Alex was not a happy bunny, very much not wanting TV cameras in our lives on a constant basis!

Part of the driver for me was to create a pictorial history of our move for my kids to show their kids of how we came to live in New Zealand – family history in the making and recorded for prosperity. So I wrote off and offered us as the Destination NZ family and amazingly we had a positive response from Colin Marchant, the MD and video creator, in-as-much-as he wanted a test tape. So it was off to the internet shops to buy a camera.

Once said camera arrived, we then took about forty "takes" to do our first three-minute piece to camera and get it sent off to Colin.

Much to our surprise he was delighted with the tape and asked us to keep going and so we had the video camera with us constantly and ran the tape whether we were happy, sad, angry or frustrated, both at home and out at play.

In the end we sent in over sixteen hours of tape, apparently significantly more than anyone else, and we had a huge amount of fun doing it all. Perhaps more importantly, it was amazing how many doors were opened when we told people we were filming for a "documentary". Also, some things seemed to suddenly get done when the camera appeared and "rolled" that seemed to have, seconds before, been a problem!

Time marched on in its inevitable way and about a week out from our supposed exchange of contracts date still nothing, so back on the phone in the middle of the night we went but could not get any commitment from NZIS or our contact as they were *busy*. Our New Zealand lawyer started to crank up his contacts in Wellington and we tracked down the email address for the head of the Business Visa Unit. A lengthy note was sent to him explaining what had happened so far, setting out our contract dates and asking for comment back as to what to expect and when. It took four or five days to get a response, which basically said he was having problems staffing his area but that he was interviewing the following week and would hopefully be able to provide a response in two or three weeks' time - no actual acknowledgement of our situation.

So, bigger guns were employed, including an approach to one of the most senior immigration officers in the service who was based in London. He sympathised big time with us and commented on how frustrated he felt that business visa applications from the UK were not dealt with in the UK. He agreed that even though they were done in New Zealand that should not have stopped them picking up the phone and talking to us about the business plan, the economics and our intentions etc. In fact, he believed that all business visa applicants should be 'interviewed'. In any event, he asked for copies of everything we had sent to Wellington and thankfully it was all stored on the computer and so off it went with a little prayer!

> *TIP:*   *Never be frightened to speak with contacts you have made or who are given to you, as you do not know what doors they can open for you. Very much in New Zealand it's as much about who you know as what you know and, once here, initially ALWAYS take every opportunity given to you to meet others, whether at a BBQ or elsewhere – you simply do not know what doors someone can open for you and this is a key part of building a support network in New Zealand.*

With still no news coming out of New Zealand, we bumped up against the exchange date. We had kept the vendors informed of the problems, as had our lawyer and they agreed to extend the date by four weeks or so. We again chased NZIS but got no response - by this time this was the expected customer service level!

Life in the UK was tense to say the least, because no matter that you know things are going on and that we had done everything asked of us we were still living the tension with every breath of every day and feeling so hopeless. We even discussed one of us jumping on a plane and sitting in the business visa office until we could have a face-to-face!

The extended exchange date came and went with nowt from New Zealand and the vendors were getting a bit restless, which was understandable. We had a completion date on the contract of the end of June and with that time up and still no response from the Business Unit to any of our emails (even from the head of the Unit) we decided to declare the contract voided (as was our right in the terms) and that we would come back and renegotiate the contract once the visa was granted. We believed that this was the fairest and most sensible approach, as it allowed the vendors certainty and took some pressure off us.

Regrettably, there was one more kick in the bum from the vendors (who, you will recall, had been 'difficult' throughout the negotiation once I was back in the UK) when we received a letter from them asking for money! We had emailed their solicitor, telling her what had happened and to ask her to send our deposit to our HSBC account in New Zealand. The next thing we know (having had no response from the lawyer) was an email letter from the vendor, suggesting we pay all their legal fees and setting out why.

Unfortunately for them, their letter was the straw that broke the proverbial camel's back and I sat down and gave them what for with all barrels. Thankfully, I was controlled enough not to send it in the heat of the moment and left it on the screen all day, reviewing it that night when calmer. It was still a hard-hitting letter and provoked the response from the vendor that a 'simple yes or no would have sufficed'. Maybe for them but not for me! I also had to write and threaten their lawyer with interest payments, as she would not move the funds into my account. Thankfully, she then moved them without further ado!

At about this time we had gone to spend some time with outstanding friends, Karen and Peter, who had this unerring habit of spotting the key issues and putting you under the spotlight until you could clearly see the way forward. This knack was invaluable and both Alex and I are immensely grateful for the friendship and enormous wisdom that both dispensed to us...and still do today!

On an earlier occasion when Alex had the "ebby-gebbies" about leaving Mum and Dad, Karen had made her sit down and think back over the past year as to how many times we had actually seen them and, of those times, how much time we spent with them and, perhaps just as importantly, had we gone to them or vice-versa? This really brought the "leaving Mum and Dad" problem into clear perspective, as it worked out at less than two weeks in a year, so what was the issue about leaving the UK? Sure, Alex had daily contact by phone but we could do similar by using MSN Messenger or SKYPE so was it appropriate to give up the dream for seeing parents less than two weeks in a year? Obviously not!

At this time, the issue was about being turned down and the key question was, what was our fall back plan if New Zealand was a non-starter? (Karen can always get to the nub of the issues!) With one look at each other and no hesitation, we both said "there is no fall back plan. We are going to New Zealand" and we both passionately believed we would. No doubts, hesitations or second thoughts – we were going to go and no bugger was going to stop us. Again, we have no idea where this level and intensity of focus came from but we sure did have it!

 ATTEMPT 2 – PERMANENT RESIDENCY

During this time we had been told by our visa agent that she had just seen someone with my financial qualifications getting points via the New Zealand Qualifications Authority (NZQA) and had subsequently applied for a Resident's Visa. So the game was on again but in a slightly different direction.

We managed to get all the necessary NZQA paperwork together and downloaded the application form from the Net.

We sent everything off via a courier to Wellington. We had paid for the express service which meant we should get a reply within ten days: you get used to the tension of waiting... honest!

Unfortunately, we did not hear back within the allotted time, so I was back on the phone in the dead of night to find out what was happening. Thankfully the NZQA were very efficient and confirmed that they had done everything and sent it off by courier. They managed to give us all the tracking details and so we were then able to get hold of the UK courier and track down our papers. It transpired that the courier had actually tried to deliver the package to us but we'd not been in, so he'd then recorded us as not in against someone else's name and address so when we initially chased they had no record of us! Needless to say, we were not impressed, but again the courier company were excellent. Not only did they send the package, they also refunded the costs of the courier service... not bad, particularly as the NZQA had given us a huge points rating: boy, I was cleverer than even I thought!

Someone was really looking out for us as I felt that my qualifications should not have rated quite so highly but, hey, you need some luck at times!

So, nearly max points on the qualification and along with other points we were almost there...I just needed a job offer. Alex put on her Internet surfing anorak and worked late into the night searching out jobs in New Zealand in financial services.

Initially, we kept bumping up against the migrants' nightmare "Catch 22", with employment/recruitment companies wanting to know my visa status. When we told them we didn't have one yet they said they couldn't help - no visa no job/no job no visa.

As you can imagine, I was rather pissed off with the seemingly intransigent attitude and let one or two companies know my feelings: here was a huge, untapped market and they seemed to be saying they could do nothing about it. This has to a degree intensified on reflection, as we are meeting people who found jobs and then got a work visa, or a work to residence visa, so why was this not offered at the time we were on the search?

In truth, now given the nature of BritsNZ's Migration business, it is still a major bug bear with us – recruitment companies are probably the worst offenders. Why advertise jobs across the Worldwide Web and then hamstring potential applicants? Either the employer for whom the Recruiter works is happy to talk with and look to employ people from off-shore or they are not and the Recruiter should react accordingly. With modern technology available, most would-be migrants can be video interviewed in their own homes and then asked to come over for interview if they look the most suitable. Sure, the lead time to that migrant actually starting work is potentially longer but it seems that Recruiters, in general, want the easy life too much.

New Zealand wants and needs migrants, both from a skill basis and to boost its tax base, and Recruiters need to get on board with the message and start earning their money, rather than taking the soft option and frustrating potential migrants and - I am sure, at times - employers!

OK, spleen vented, so back to the story!
Eventually we knew we needed to rationalise our search pattern and try to hit companies directly. To do this we found a list of advisers on the New Zealand Financial Advisers Association website and then turned to the Internet Yellow Pages. I scribed a letter and we attached that and my CV to emails and quantified my qualifications according to the information given to us by the NZQA.

We further refined the search by thinking where we'd like to go, and here we thought of Taranaki/New Plymouth. We'd seen their stand and video at the Emigrate Fair (interestingly, it never rained on their video!) and had listened to the Mayor speak at a seminar and met him (one giant of a Kiwi - I got a crick in my neck trying to look him in the eye), so that formed one of our initial search centres.

It was not long before we got a reply and so off we went to the phones again and started talking about a job.

With our conversations and emails flowing, a job offer followed and we were able to submit a general skills permanent residency application...yipeeeee! All that hard work and stress seemed to be coming to an end.

Having been here once before with application forms, we pulled the appropriate ones off the Net, completed them and then sent them off to our Visa Agents, as they had offered to check it all again for us prior to submission. There were one or two things they suggested we add.

TIP: *Double – no, triple – check that you have not only the right form but also the most up-to-date one – I had completed nearly all five applications when, by chance, I realised the form was not current – I was not a happy chappy!*

Whilst all this was happening we were calling in favours to see if our now just out-of-date medicals (they last three months) and police checks (they last six months) could still be used. They could, thank goodness, particularly with regard to the medicals, as we did not want to fork out another £500 - but I made sure to include a letter from my GP, confirming that none of the family had been in to see him since we underwent our medicals. We then spent some time with Bruce Burrows, the senior man at Immigration in London, as I was insistent that we do this in person, because I didn't want anything else to go wrong. Bruce came up trumps: I spoke to the head of the London Visa Unit and we booked a time to go up and see her.

We got all our papers together in a presentation file, thinking that would be a big plus in that everything would be really clear and in some form of order. We also took a briefcase full of all and any paper we thought they could conceivably want. This proved good foresight, as they did ask for a couple of things which we had with us. We were introduced to a Unit Manager, who had a brief look and then introduced us to the officer who would take our application all the way through. We had a lengthy chat with her and took her through our file.

We were pleased that we had taken the opportunity to take the file there ourselves and that we had taken the video along for the diary we were creating. We left knowing we had done the absolute best we could and so were back in the wait zone...we were expecting it to be about four weeks. We had actually been asked when we needed a response and I had, somewhat tongue in cheek, said, "Oh, next week will be fine", which had elicited a rueful smile which I took to mean maybe not!

On returning home, we found a message waiting to say that the credit card payment had been declined. Hearts sank and blood pressure rose, as we knew there was not an issue with the card. On the phone to the credit card company we found that they were cracking down on payments to postal addresses such as the NZIS address was classed and, as they had not got hold of me to verify the payment, had declined it. I told them what to expect and went back to NZIS to get them to re-do. They appreciated the reason for the decline and were cool about it.

The conundrum then was what to do next, as by now we were very suspicious of doing anything ahead of time just in case it put a jinx on things! In any event I needed to sort out my other work, as we were off to Devon the following week for a holiday.

 THE LONG-AWAITED MOMENT

The day we were setting off on holiday we ended up leaving later than planned, as kids/Mum couldn't get their backsides into gear, and I happened to be loading final bits into the car when the postie arrived.

In amongst all our other mail was a large, thick A4 envelope with Immigration New Zealand stamped on the back...my heart was racing and doing somersaults at the same time – of course this being only eight days after we delivered our application there was real fear that it was a further rejection. I can still feel the emotion of it even now as I write this.

The sun was shining, we were about to go on holiday and I was caught between desperately wanting to know what was in the letter and being petrified to open the damned thing! With my heart thumping I decided to say nothing to anyone else and opened the envelope.

I remember taking the letter out with my eyes closed – what that did for me, I have no idea - but when I did open my eyes and read the letter I had to re-read it to make sure it was true...bloody hell! We had been granted Permanent Residency – no surely my eyes needed testing – no it really, really was true!

I bounded up the stairs and dragged Alex out of the shower to read the letter. Whilst she did that, I sat on the loo and cried - too much tension over too long a period. We had finally made it. We were just so elated!

Alex immediately got on the phone to her mum to break the news and I promptly filmed her soaking wet in just a towel telling her mum. All was huge excitement until Alex said she had to go as she was all but naked, to which her mum said she was, too – talk about information overload!

We then thought about cancelling our holiday, but as Devon was so very special to me we decided to go ahead and start saying goodbye to places and people...and, of course, have that last Devon cream tea – ah, clotted cream! Everyone we told was so pleased for us and truly shared our relief and excitement, although there was a hint of sadness, knowing we would be saying goodbye to them at some stage.

 LEAVING THE UK

After the euphoria of finally having the visa and setting off for a "last" holiday in the UK to one of our favourite places, it was not long until it sank in that one bridge crossed meant another steaming up on the horizon, and one that would be as difficult as getting the visas – actually getting out of the UK.

Trust me when I say that whilst for many getting a visa is a very trying time and, when completed, it is very easy to think the hard bit is done, but I think actually packing up and leaving the UK is as hard, if not harder. Certainly the emotional stresses go into hyper-drive and of course you are faced by multiple upon multiple of decisions, from which way to fly down to New Zealand to what to take and what to leave behind.

For us the main initial decision was just how soon to leave, as that would dictate costs and timings of flights and when to give notice on our rental property in the UK...and when to resign from my job. For reasons I'm not sure I now remember very well, we aimed to leave at the end of September and that was probably in an effort to tie in with the last school term of the year in New Zealand, so that we could give the kids some settling time and time to make some friends before the summer holidays over Christmas. (See? Already totally different and something that has probably only now started to tune in – all the seasons being reversed!)

This timeline gave us effectively six weeks to pack up and ship out...I am utterly hopeless at lists. They drive me bonkers. But Alex is a star with them and I am the first to admit that this is a time when lists are an absolute MUST – there is simply just too much to do to efficiently do it all through memory recall.

By the end of those six weeks I was almost standing to attention at the end of the bed each morning awaiting my daily orders, but I am very thankful that we did work in this way as we managed to get done nearly everything we needed to do and left little of any consequence undone. You always need to bear in mind that what you don't get done before leaving will then need to be done from another time zone and, in New Zealand's case, from t'other side of the world, so it all becomes a little more difficult, which tends to focus the mind somewhat.

Through the nature of our business (UK Pension Transfers) we call companies in the UK and make it plain we are calling from New Zealand only to be asked if they can call us back "later". Many times people seem a little put out when you say "no" until you explain (usually very s_l_o_w_l_y!) that a call back at 2 p.m. UK time is 2 a.m. Kiwi time and that you really do not wish to be awakened! We have learnt that we should not assume that people in the UK can readily understand or know the time difference. So, the key is a very clear focus on getting done what must be done before you fly out!

Bearing in mind our previous "false start" we already had a series of quotes in from removals companies, but by this time we had come across other providers we wanted to look at and I think in the end had something like six or seven quotes to wade through – trust me that is way too many!

TIP: *Get no more than three quotes for moving and aim to get those done between six and three months before you leave.*

Whilst the "bottom line" is important it is actually more important to listen to your gut – you are inviting strangers into your house to pack everything you have worked so hard to accumulate and you need to feel comfortable with having these people in your home.

Before they come to quote, walk the house, sit in the loft, pick through the garage and identify what you do not want to take with you. Once the removal companies have been in and quoted, you may want to go through the process again and perhaps look to leave more behind depending on the size of container they quote.

By doing this early(ish) you give yourself a chance to sell (through free ads in the local papers, on your supermarket notice boards, through on-line sites and at car boot sales) what you are not taking and generate some additional funds to help you move. Alex managed to generate over £1,000 in this manner so it can be well worth it!

The key here is knowing that all your electrical goods will work in New Zealand, as we are on the same power usage as the UK and it is simply a question of changing plugs, so there are no issues about white goods etc...but it will be different in different countries.

We know a number of people who have simply arrived in New Zealand with their suitcases, having sold, given away or dumped what they had in the UK in order to "start again" in New Zealand. I have yet to find one who reflectively thinks that this was a good idea. I mean, simply walk around your home and start estimating the cost of replacing everything you already own and remember how long it took you to accumulate all your possessions, and then ask yourself whether you should take everything or not...TAKE IT!

Also remember, especially if you have kids, that you are all going to be foreigners in a foreign, unfamiliar land and some six to eight weeks after you leave behind everything you know, having familiar things around you is a real bonus and is an anchor which helps you settle!

I well remember videoing the unpacking of our stuff in New Zealand and seeing Gabs with a small pile of her favourite videos in her hand from a box, looking for a TV to watch them on – the look of happiness on her little face was/is priceless and was crucial at that time!

Further, once you have estimated the cost of everything you own, think (and be realistic here) what you could get for it on the second hand market and then start looking at shipping costs: a twenty-foot container will currently (2008/9) set you back between £3,000 and £4,000 and I would suggest that this is money well spent when you look at how much value you have in your house currently, the time and effort it took you to accumulate it all and the help it will give you to settle. It is definitely worth bringing it all with you!

Of course, it's not just the possessions you need to sort out, it's all that lovely paperwork you have accumulated over so many years – what to do with it all?

Naturally, you will need to bring some with you in your suitcase and even some in your container, but ultimately it's bonfire/shredding time!

To be fair, by this stage of your emigration it is somewhat late to be considering what your financial needs may be, but if you have not done so by now then it becomes critical to do so! In my opinion, I must re-iterate that sorting out your finances must rank up there with sorting out your visas.

Ultimately, whilst you may feel you know sufficient about most aspects of your finances, there will be much that you should seek advice on before leaving the UK, not only in respect of what to do with it as you are leaving but also as to how moving to New Zealand impacts. In this respect, you need to search out people who can advise over both jurisdictions. These are the key areas where you should be looking to seek advice (from really nice people like us!):

- A review of your current UK circumstances
- Preferential dealings with a currency exchange specialist
- Setting up New Zealand bank accounts more simply
- Advice on what to do with your UK bank account(s)
- Professional advice relating to your UK pensions
- Knowledge and insights about the pension transfer process
- Maximisation of your UK investments
- Advice on everyday tax issues – income tax and tax on UK bank accounts
- Advice on how to minimise your Capital Gains and Inheritance Tax liabilities
- Explanations of how to take advantage of your New Zealand new migrant allowances
- Advice on how best to set up your wills
- Repatriation insurance

I am actually a specialist in this area with twenty-five plus years in Financial Services in the UK (ten of those as a front line adviser) and have been an IFA here in New Zealand for over five years. I, therefore, have an in-depth knowledge of both the UK and New Zealand systems and can thus more fully advise people.

Quite rightly, most people focus on getting their visas (and a job) as their key priority but I am here to tell you that whilst you cannot come and live and work in New Zealand without the visa, right alongside it in importance is sorting your finances. The longer you look at this aspect, the better planned your move will be and you will be giving yourselves an enhanced ability to settle successfully. There is little point in getting to New Zealand and then being in difficulties simply through lack of financial planning.

With regard to our own move, for instance, whilst I could do most everything myself as my focus was on getting the family to New Zealand, I knew I could not give the time and attention to sorting out a key asset of ours, my pension benefits. I actually chose (much to Alex's disgust) to go to a third party to look into my pension benefits, recommend a course of action and then to get on and manage that process. Of course, I was fortunate in that I understood fully the process and what information was supplied but to me it was money well spent, as I would not have given this very important asset the care and attention it needed. So you see even I learned when to look for help, given the amount of things we needed to do!

By this time in our move we would literally ask for something out loud and wait for it to be given and such was the case with opening a bank account. I happened to be speaking with an old friend who worked internationally for HSBC and mentioned my move to New Zealand. Lo and behold, another old school contact happened to work for them in Auckland and, hey presto, we soon had accounts open and waiting for funds. I have to say the process of opening accounts for new migrants here in New Zealand before they arrive is amazingly simple and that simplicity makes your lives so much easier. You have all you need to hand in the UK to open an account and then once in New Zealand it's simply a case of going into the bank with your ID and there it all is ready to go!

Again, writing lists is a must as there is just so much paperwork to sort out and organise. You have things to stop, other things to keep but re-direct and the clock is continually ticking down! We opted to have everything re-directed to Alex's mum, who is herself well organised and who kept us fully up-to-date with what arrived in the post. Needless to say that from the other side of the world a lot of it was classed as junk and we often wondered why we had never registered it as such whilst living in the UK!

There are always the regular things you instantly recognise you need to deal with; gas, electric, phone, banks etc – but of course there will be a myriad of other things; sports club membership, magazine subscriptions, wine clubs, book clubs etc, etc, and it takes time and effort to both remember and actually close all these things down. Naturally, once identified, a "standard letter" will suffice, but it does all take time.

Then, of course, you want/need to pry your medical records away from your GP. This is very important, particularly with kids in tow, as it helps to arrive in your new country with some detailed medical records (and in the kids' cases, their immunisation history) so that your care can be better managed. GPs in the UK are a tad reluctant at times to give you copies of your records but under the Data Protection Act they must do so on request, although they may charge you for the copies – but it's worth the cost!

So there we were with the clock ticking, trying to get all this sorted and reviewing regularly where we were and making sure we'd not forgotten anything – this was Alex's area and as I said I simply stood by my bed each day awaiting orders!

I think it is fair to say, though, that the most difficult thing is getting ready for the removal guys, as you are constantly looking at things and wondering whether you really do need to take it with you and whether you have been told by the removers that you can't take it. Much to my disgust they insisted that I could not take my wine with me – I was all for saying, "Sod it" and taking it anyway but Alex was insistent that I not take it. I had taken considerable time, effort and expense in building my "cellar" and it was heartbreaking to not be able to take it with me.

However, we managed to drink some of it and the rest I made sure went to good homes!

As soon as we had identified the date by which we would leave we did two things. We gave more than the required notice period with our landlord, partly because he was working in Germany and we wanted to give him the ability to come back and see the property if he so wished. In fact, he opted to put the house on the market which was fine except that the flaming estate agent was hopeless and we kept having people turn up by themselves for viewings. This had a real impact on our time, and no amount of nagging to the manager of the Agency changed that so we simply gave up and showed people around!

I also opted to resign my job earlier than perhaps was necessary but thought it only fair. Once Scottish Widows realised that I was not off to a competitor they opted to "accept" my resignation from the day I flew out to New Zealand. The importance of this was that we were left with the company car right up until the time I left and, in reality, generated me extra income. Okay, I still had to answer the phone and see a client if they called and wanted a meeting, but that was not a high price to pay. I simply cannot thank Scottish Widows and my colleagues enough for taking this amazing decision and giving me on-going support, because it was simply a massive help to us. Thank you!

Alex was also very insistent that we did not have a going away party – she felt very strongly that this would just have been far too emotional a thing to do, so we compromised by giving her an early 40th birthday party and she seemed happy to disguise the fact that it was a leaving party in this way. In any event, we had a brilliant night and managed to see almost everyone we loved and cared about. Certainly we had sore heads the next day, but having a house full of people meant we took a break from the daily grind of leaving, which was absolutely necessary and we would suggest the same for anyone else. In amongst all you have to do to leave you do need to create some "you" time and some fun time!

TIP: *Try to bring people to you and NOT charge around the country seeing all and sundry – hence a "leaving party" of some sort makes sense. Believe me whilst people will want to say "goodbye and fare-thee-well" they will tend to want to do so on their terms – i.e. you travel to them! You will be exhausted by simply leaving so try not to over do things – if people won't come to you so be it!*

Whilst initially we felt that Alex's mum and dad were being very supportive we knew this move would be difficult for her dad who, being Greek, was coming at this from a different cultural angle.

We had never kept our plans secret from anyone, bar my then employer, and we would urge all would be migrants to do likewise. This is a tough one and we never cease to be surprised by the number of people who are reluctant to tell their parents of their plans for "fear" of upsetting them and/or who do not include their kids all the way through the process: having the kids on board (as much as is possible for them) from Day One is VITAL!

The point is that if the parents get upset, its better that they do so some time away from you leaving rather than really close – they need to get used to the idea and, trust me, you will want/need their support as departure day approaches.

The key thing is that as long as you hold firm as to why you are doing this and what the drivers are, quite simply if other people don't get it that's their problem, not yours. Try hard not to let anyone who is being negative about your move get you down and certainly be very careful of listening too hard to advice from people who have neither migrated nor been to the country to which you are going. Ask yourself this – how do they know that what they are saying is correct? The answer is of course that they don't know and it is just emotion talking.

In our case, things headed south for a while once we had the visas and it was obvious that we had been serious all along. That is when we got the subtle "have this as your inheritance as I will not see you again" from Alex's Dad along with bold and loud protestations that he would NEVER come and see us and what about his grandchildren. All this from a man who lived less than an hour and a half from us and who came to see us less than eight times in eight years – sure, we would see them fairly regularly but that was because we made the effort.

Needless to say this had quite a profound effect on Alex at times and not only did it threaten our plans it also put a huge pressure on our marriage. So much so, in fact, that in the end I bundled everyone in the car and we went to see them, when I had to point out quite forcefully that come hell or high water we were going to New Zealand and they could either enjoy the time before departure with us and the kids or we simply would stop seeing and speaking with them!

Thankfully, the light was seen and some kind of harmony returned. We all, but especially the kids, had some fun time with their grandparents and they were incredibly helpful in the final few weeks.

Since being here, Alex's mum has been out for a few months and as I write this we are a few weeks away from her dad coming out – the kids don't know and they will be blown away when he arrives. From Alex's point of view it's about him coming and seeing and not about how long he stays – hopefully he will stay a while, but we are just happy he has opted to come and see what we have created for ourselves.

Whilst on this subject, and it is something that will come up in the lead up to departure, is the question of when people should come and visit and when you are likely to take a trip back. Our advice is this (and we acknowledge there is no right or wrong way but this is simply our experience and that of our clients):

- Parents, family and friends to you – not for the first year at least. And always remember that they will be coming on holiday, whilst you will potentially be working and you need to manage expectations and time accordingly!

- You back to the UK – not for a minimum of eighteen months, and ideally not in the first two years, except if you do get very unsettled (or more importantly and usually) if teenage kids are not settling in. Perhaps then a trip back to remember what you left behind and reflect on what you now have can make the difference to you settling. But if you can stick to the two years then it will be to your advantage.

In saying the above, we know that there will be tough times and homesickness will potentially rear its head – to be fair it is uncommon to find migrants who simply fall straight into life and have none of these feelings – and our advice at that time is get out of the house and go somewhere special (beach, bush, mountain etc) and look around you. Remember why you left and what it is you have here and, most importantly, do NOT beat yourself up about feeling homesick, it is completely normal for most of us!

We actually had to put off Alex's mum coming in the first year and in fact we felt quite unsettled when she came after one year – nothing personal but it did unsettle the settling in – if you know what I mean! We also went back after eighteen months, more because we were invited to speak at various Emigration Shows, and with the company just launched we needed to take the opportunity, but we were worried about going, particularly as we opted to take the kids. As it happens, it was a turning point for our eldest, who came back a changed kid – he won't ever admit that, but certainly school reports changed for the better!

As I said no real right or wrong!

So, the time marched on and the rationalising of our things carried on apace. I must admit to becoming a little worried at one point when I went out a meeting: I came back an hour and a half later and as I strode into the house I threw my files on the dining room table. I heard a very strange noise and it was at this point I realised we no longer had the table. I did then ask Alex whether we still had a bed to sleep in as I would have put nothing past "Mrs Focused" by that point!

This was also the time for the monotony of cleaning, cleaning and sterilising/disinfecting all our stuff, and particularly the outdoor stuff. New Zealand is particularly neurotic (and quite rightly so) about anything undesirable entering the country so it was necessary to make sure everything was perfect. Thankfully, Alex's dad was back "on-side" with the move by then and he came over with his industrial steam cleaner and cleaned everything in sight – in fact it got dangerous to stand and watch for risk of being steam cleaned too! It was at times like this that we wondered why we had so much stuff and why it was all coming with us, and the only saving grace was that we were not having to pack everything ourselves, but there was still a whole heap of things to clear out and sort.

Again, all the praise must go to Alex who organised things fantastically. What was not being given away needed to be sold and she either worked on Amazon or used free ads in the local papers, cards in the local Tesco and car boot sales. This is not my area at all and one car boot sale was more than enough for me: as we parked the car, a swarm of locusts descended on us and started to actually take stuff out the car and were simply bloody rude – very definitely not my idea of fun. Thankfully, the kids liked it so they tended to go with her, but there were times that I was concerned that more came back than went out when the kids were in tow!

By the time we left she had amassed more than the cost of one air ticket and all power to her – she was quite simply brilliant!

When we had looked at the removals quotes all had said we would need just over a twenty-foot container and our removals company, PSS International, still held to that idea when they turned up to start the packing process. We were, however, quietly confident that Alex had slimmed our belongings sufficiently, but we still took the precaution of identifying what should go on last so if it didn't make it then we'd not be too upset!

TIP: *Clear the clutter.*
       Look to sell what you are not taking with you –
       make some additional money!
       Identify what can be packed in the container
       last so if it doesn't go in it won't matter overly to
       you!

The first of two packing days duly arrived and the PSS team descended on us. This was initially almost unbearable for Alex (and, dare I say, for most of our lady migrants), because she could do nothing – she could not pack a thing or it would potentially invalidate the insurance...however she did make up for this by being as bossy as possible – she got to know how far she could push them when the request for a cuppa was made!

Anyway, the PSS boys turned up and I took them on a tour of the property, pointing out what was going and what needed to be last "just in case". The tour ended in the garage, where one of the sharper-eyed packers asked what I intended for the three cases of beer in the corner, to which I said, "We have been told you cannot get everything into a twenty-foot container. That beer is to help you focus on proving them wrong – get it all in and it's all yours!" Well, you got to give an incentive when you need to do so!

I have to say that PSS were simply amazing – the speed at which they packed was mind boggling and we were very pleased that we'd heeded the advice to remove everything from the house that we needed for our trip or it would have gone. There are numerous stories of tickets and passports ending up in the container and in need of rescue. In fact, a good friend of ours opened his container in New Zealand to find his UK next door neighbour's trailer had come to New Zealand with him: he'd had to pop out at the "wrong" moment. He said the resulting phone call back to the UK was very amusing!

So, the end of day one of The PSS Big Pack saw us all sleeping on mattresses on the floor amongst boxes and our things that we could no longer recognise due to the way they had been packed – our sofas definitely no longer looked like sofas!

I should add that I am sure the only reason at least one child did not end up in the container was because the boys were at school and Gabs was off with friends.

So, Day Two of the PSS Big Pack dawned and with it the arrival of the container on the back of a very large lorry, which we managed to get close to the house with not too much disruption to all the neighbours! That day also saw the arrival of Nick Witham, the MD of PSS, to take some photos of the work in process. He wandered around looking at everything that needed to go (asked the same question about the beer and laughed out loud when I explained the incentive) and had just commented that he was convinced we'd not get it all into the container when a friend turned up and said, "I have the kayak for you to take to New Zealand". Nick's face paled, but by then we were past caring. We helped our friend get the kayak off his car and laid the new challenge in front of the PSS team!

Eventually, our precious possessions started to disappear into the container and watching the guys stack and pack it was amazing – it was like watching someone complete a 3D jigsaw – poetry in motion and spatial awareness.

At one point late in the day with the lorry driver eager to get going and space running short I went in the house to see five guys trying to manhandle a wardrobe down the stairs. Now you'd expect them to be all professional but one made a crazy comment and they all dissolved in laughter and all instantly lost their strength – you know exactly what I mean! I suggested that I should make some tea whilst they try and figure out how to get it down the stairs. That was when I had a moment of total clarity and wandered back out to say to the guys, "Would it help to know that I assembled the wardrobe in the bedroom and it's never been up the stairs whole?" They stopped and stared at me and almost as one said "Mike, you plonker!" But every cloud has a silver lining, as they effectively then flat-packed the whole thing and we just, literally just, managed to get everything in and the door shut...yes, including that kayak!

Now, if you have read this far, the following will sound more than a little bizarre. When those container doors shut and the truck disappeared around the corner it was an intensely emotional time for me as, at that moment, it all became totally real for me: we were really leaving the UK and fulfilling the dream and I was, for about half an hour, an emotional wreck. Why that moment created the reality for me I have no idea, but I suppose I was at a point where there was so little to do but wait out the next five days before we left. Or perhaps the physicality of seeing all our possession disappear was a trigger. Anyway, that was the situation and thankfully Alex, whilst not being so affected, understood the situation and was a brick for me. (Actually, just recounting this now, I can feel the emotion of it and feel the tears pricking the backs of my eyes. In fact, that is something that I seem to be able to do with comparative ease – put myself back in that emotional state by talking about it – it's like it's happening now!)

I well remember how we both felt on that first trip back to speak at the Emigrate seminars. Alex is not happy speaking in front of a whole host of people, whilst I totally love it, feel completely at ease and love projecting the passion I feel for the subject matter!

On the first session of the seminars Alex just froze, bless her. She was asked a question and simply could not get any words out but after ten minutes with me chatting and making her and the audience laugh she realised she actually had all the answers and settled into it like a pro and the other sessions went really well. Until, that was, the Sunday session, by which time I was exhausted!

A specific clip was shown and the exhaustion took me straight back with all the pent up emotions (heck, I can feel it again right now – compose yourself Coley!) and I simply sat there with tears falling, unable to get the words out and - bless her - Alex rode to the rescue by looking at me and then saying the immortal words to about a hundred and fifty people, "Ah bless. He's crying". She then looking up at the audience said, "Well, so are many of you!" which thankfully broke the spell and caused some laughter and I found my voice again. It was, though totally unintentional, a real insight for people as to just how much an emotional roller coaster emigrating will be for most people at some point.

I think the key here is that you simply accept that at some point(s) you will get very emotional and you should be "happy" with that as it is entirely to be expected and most everyone will go through it and so do not beat yourself up about it. Simply live the moment and, with the support of your husband/wife/kids/family/friends, embrace it, ride it, understand it in others, allow it to flow out from you and then carry on.

So, where was I? Oh yes, the house is now empty apart from what we need to take to the outlaws, and it is time to do the major clean ready for the agent's inspection. One area of concern was the room where Gabriella and her little friend, Izzy, had managed, just two days before, to pour touch-up paint onto a cream carpet. We had dashed out and got a carpet cleaning machine and had "washed" it about four times and whilst there was just, literally just, a discernable stain in the sunlight, we felt we had done okay and got it pretty much perfect!

At this time Scottish Widows had arranged for my company car to be picked up and given that we were about ready to leave for the outlaws it seemed fine to let it go then. Well, that was until I looked at just what we were planning on taking to Mum and Dad's and realised that we'd not get it and all of us into our car (which we were leaving for Alex's dad to sell for us).

I walked back into the kitchen and explained this to Alex and said "one of us has to go to Mum and Dad's now and come back, or we could do with the company car not going now!" Well, twenty minutes later (I absolutely swear it was no longer than that), the Angels delivered as my mobile rang and a young lady said:

"Hi this is the company coming to pick up the company car."
"Oh. You can't find the house, can you?" says I.
"No, that's not it. The man meant to pick up the car has had to rush home, his daughter has been taken poorly and we need to reschedule the pick up."

Well, talk about goose bumps and hair standing up on the back of necks – we asked and it was delivered and whilst by this time it was not a major surprise, the speed with which this particular need/request was answered was mind boggling.

My next words to the lady on the phone were, "You are an absolute Angel and have answered a major issue from us," to which she said, "You are the very first person who has actually said anything nice to me all day. Thank you!" - "My dear girl, then this is a sign to you – go home for the rest of the day whilst you are ahead!" says I!

Anyway, the outcome was that we arranged for the car to be picked up from the outlaws the following week, so one major problem was resolved!

The next was the agent's inspection, which we did not expect to be a problem as we had kept the house meticulously clean and tidy and, indeed, it appeared to pass off fine. Until, that is we got to standing in the airport on Monday morning and the agent decided that he wanted the carpets cleaned again – note I said agent and NOT landlord (who was selling the house in any event) – the agent had been a pain all the way through and was now insistent that it be done "professionally" – did he know someone? Of course he did, but then so did we, so Alex's Dad was dispatched to clean it again and then all was well with the carpet...mind, we then had to contact the landlord directly by e-mail to get our bond back as the agent was having a problem – not for long!

That night we were spending our last night with friends before leaving for Alex's mum and dad's and it just so happened that there was a traditional beer festival on our village green that night. I had arranged to meet loads of people there as a bit of a farewell do –

quite fitting to finish our lives in Essex with great people around us, drinking traditional British ale!

The next morning was quite emotional saying goodbye to Gus and Linds Hellier and their kids. They had become such an intrinsic part of our lives, always round drinking my wine and helping create mayhem in the kitchen as I created something for us all to eat and who often wobbled off on bikes back home with too much wine and food on board!

Friends like these guys don't come around that often and our heartfelt thanks go out to them for all the help and support they gave us, particularly with our New Zealand move – guys you were awesome, thank you!

Now you see it now you don't! The great team from PSS
International Removals pack the lounge.

The container stands open and waiting to take all our
possessions to NZ – September 2003

Us watching the 3-D jigsaw of packing a container take shape – an amazing job extremely well done by the PSS team!

So, we were nearly gone from the UK and were still filming away for the DVD diary, but that last day/night with Alex's mum and dad was quite hard – hard, as we were trying to keep emotions in check whilst watching the clock count down to the unknown. Oh, we had no doubts, but as many will know the waiting is often worse than the action itself! After one particular conversation with my Oz-based sister, I had decided that we would spend the last night in the UK at a hotel at Heathrow and NOT have anyone see us off at the gate. Both Alex and I realised that the emotion of saying goodbye and then climbing into a plane in some degree of distress would not be clever and would be very hard on all of us.

So, at the due time on the Sunday afternoon, a taxi turned up and many tear was shed by Alex and Joe and the family and it was heartbreaking to see Alex's dad with tears pouring down his face. (Hold on - here come those emotions back again! I am writing this as I fly up to the UK for another set of shows and thankfully have no one next to me to see the emotions coming and going, but trust me they are real!) and also to see Alex and Joe in some distress. Thankfully, Jake seemed immune from it and was genuinely puzzled as to why his big bro and mum were in floods of tears, whilst Gabs, bless her heart simply sat in her car seat silently looking on and occasionally smiling at her mum!

Interestingly, amongst all the tears, one event was a bit of shock to us. As Alex hugged her sister goodbye, she had whispered to Alex, "Well, thanks very much for leaving Mum and Dad to me to look after by myself." The problem was that she'd not been joking and it was a bitter disappointment to hear that, especially as we had done so much whilst we had been in the UK. We had never intended to abdicate helping with Mum and Dad, whether that was physically by Alex coming back as, when and if needed and/or supplying funds as needed, so it was a bit of a cold bucket of water and, in my opinion, totally unwarranted. As it turned out, it was a precursor for issues in the future – but enough said here!

Thankfully, we had opted for a hotel with a pool, spa and sauna and so once we had managed to get all our luggage into our room – how the hell I was going to get all of it to New Zealand I did not at that time know! – we were in the pool and chilling with the kids and thanking our decision to do this. It helped wash away those emotions from earlier in the day and gave us valuable down time as a small family unit.

TIP: *No matter which airport you leave from stay the night before departure nearby in an hotel and do not have people to see you off at the departure gate!*

We had planned to have friends Karen and Peter come and see us for supper but good old problems on motorways stopped that happening. However, we still had a nice relaxed evening and Karen turned up for breakfast. So much for my above tip, eh? But she was a god-send and helped with the kids and getting us to the airport in some semblance of order the next day!

Departure day arrives and we have a cruisey morning and head off on the airport bus early as we knew getting through the checking in and through customs and security would take the five of us sometime. We had also arranged to meet Colin Marchant so that he could do some live filming and get a live interview before we left. He was treading a thin line as, after 9/11, security was suspicious of a film unit in an airport, but that all went quite well until the point at which we were checking in and being filmed. The poor check-in guy got totally flustered with the camera rolling and managed to cock up the tagging of the bags. They were all meant to go through to New Plymouth (we had opted to take an internal flight in New Zealand to simply get us there as quickly as possible) and he had done some but not all. However, he assured us, both at the check-in desk and again at the departure gate, that he would get it all tagged correctly!

Whilst we were going through the check-in procedure, Joe had been on his mobile to his school mates during their lunch break and that brief period of time saw him change from being positive about the move to being a nightmare about it and at times a nasty nightmare about it. Little did we know then that it would last about two years..!

TIP: *When you leave home that final time whether it's to an airport hotel or to the airport turn off all the mobiles (yes, all of them, no exceptions) and do not turn them on again until you arrive at your final destination. We realised too late that for Joe it was just like having his friends sitting right next to him – a bitter lesson to learn, judging by what followed!*

We had opted to fly down to New Zealand using Air New Zealand and at that time the only real option had been to go through LA, as that guaranteed us a bigger luggage allowance. What we know now is that most airlines flying into New Zealand will offer you more luggage allowance if you personally call them about two weeks before departure and let them have a copy of your visa. The only ones we are aware of at this time who can be a little difficult are Emirates!

So, it was with a sense of excitement (and a little fear and apprehension) that we finally stepped on the plane and left the UK on our way to making a dream a reality!

I think it is worth pointing out here that as far as we are concerned we are just ordinary people who did something extraordinary. I think that is very true of any migrant and for sure, if we can do it then anyone can with the right amount of focus and determination and a will to never be put off and, equally importantly, to see things as a challenge to rise to as opposed to a problem!

Without doubt, doing the video diary has been a bonus not just in capturing some special family history but also in what doors it's opened and what amazing things it has led to. We could never have foreseen some six years ago that an ordinary couple with three kids living in heartland Essex would leave the UK bound for New Zealand; that we would end up creating a video diary seen by thousands; appear in the centre pages of the Sunday Times Magazine; appear on national New Zealand radio and TV; and create a company which allowed us to pass on the passion for our new country and which would afford us the privilege of helping other people realise their dreams!

Photographed for the Taranaki Daily News
October 2003. This was then used as the cover
for the Emigrate Challenge DVD

Joe & Jake coming back up the Luge chairlift to race
down to the bottom again. Rotorua, November 2003

A month into NZ and visiting Rotorua's local park to see the steam and bubbling mud- note the stout "barrier" separating us from the hot mud.

Now 18, Joe at 13 on his mother's 40th birthday fancy dress party – December 2003

PART 4

THE FIRST YEAR – THE LETTERS HOME

Whilst looking at what to include in this, our first book, we decided to cover up to the end of the first year and to comment on a couple of other key things.

When looking at that first year, the obvious place to start was with the letters I had written home. We then thought, why not simply use them as the basis of letting you "into" our first year, since this is the "raw emotion", if you will, of what we experienced. We are taking the liberty to add some reflective comment at the end of each letter to give you our view on what we feel in the "now".

So here is our first year in New Zealand...

LETTER 1 HOME – 15 OCTOBER 2003

'A very big HI and G'DAY to all who knows us (and even those who have forgotten us already! Bastards!)

We have now been in NZ for two weeks, but, boy, does it feel longer. That's probably because for the first week we were waking/getting up around 3 am with the jet lag...we are really only now just about over that so normalcy is returning!

We had pretty good flights all the way through although, in reality, both legs were just too long for the kids, who were actually really good.10.15hrs down to LA and then 12.30 hrs to Auckland...very tiring and somewhat boring. Gabs had a bit of an abdab as we taxied out to take off from LA (by which time it would have been 7am in the UK and she was well tired). I was sitting next to a woman who said "can't someone put that kid on the wing..." to which I of course said "that's my little girl" much to the lady's embarrassment. We were all very tired by that time so I forgave her and she later shared her Ferrero Roche chocys with me...not a bad trade!

We were late leaving London and that carried on through the flight, so we were being pushed to catch our internal flight in any event and then disaster struck...three bags were missing...We subsequently found that they had been left in London: the check-in man had felt the pressure of our video diary and being filmed by us and the chap we are doing the Video Diary for and managed to send some bags to Auckland and some through to New Plymouth (NP). It was critical to have it tagged to NP so we would not have excess luggage probs on the internal leg. He had to "run downstairs and change the tickets on the bags" and then assured us at the gate that all was done...we know his name - he's a marked man!

The outcome with the luggage was that we were on the phone at 2.30 the next morning (NZ time), talking to Karen to give them hell in London and get the bags sent. We eventually got the bags the following day... big prob was that we realised in the middle of the night that one of the missing bags had all our bank details including passwords (!!!) Don't ask me why ask 'er indoors!

We managed to get on the internal flight... just. We had to run from the international terminal to the internal one - that was about a mile. We had all the luggage that had arrived, Gabs was in her jimjams and it was raining heavily. We then got to the gate and they managed to hold an already delayed flight for us, but initially the only person logged on was Gabs. Kept hearing a tannoy announcement asking "Miss Cole to pls board the plane"... bye Gabs!

We managed to squeeze on, which led to a dash across the tarmac in pouring rain to board a plane with everyone in their business suits looking bemused as a posse of Brits came on shaking off water and apologising for the further delay. This was a tiny plane, a thirty-seater, and full.

Jake and I sat together and his first question was "What is that thing on the wing?" It was a propeller.

This fascinated Jake until they ran the engine to full power and it 'disappeared', to which he said "oh no! It's fallen off!"

The flight was uneventful. It took thirty-five mins to get down to NP and boy when I say down I mean down as in like a roller coaster! Nothing if not a little exciting!

As we got off the plane the heavens open and a hail storm followed. As I got to the door, a chap stood there in a Sou'wester and said "welcome to NP"....I nearly said "actually I'm going back"....but just jumped out and ran for it!

We met the guy and girl I'm working with and they managed to get us to the motel and then out for breakfast with a trip round NP, which did not take too long! And then back to motel...boy oh boy, we were really cold and are still waiting to warm up. They say that since we got here they are having the worst of the winter weather...bloody typical! Joe went to bed about midday and slept seventeen straight hours to the next morning...the others did very well but were up and ready to go by 4 am next morning!

NP is a small town with the sea on one side and a bloody big mountain on the other. The mountain is a bit shy and does not come out to play often but when it does it is breathtakingly lovely with the sun shining on a snow-capped peak...awesome!

The locals worry about getting around town but in all seriousness we can get from one extreme end to t'other in no more than ten to twelve mins and similarly from top to bottom...and there is no such thing as a traffic jam...we still can't see what the locals are worrying about!

The boys are both in school. Joe is at Devon Intermediate School for this term and then will go up to Spotswood College (the only co-ed school in NP) in January. Luckily it appears that most of his class will also be going up so he will know a bunch of kids. He has an English guy as his teacher, who happens to support Arsenal (poor bugger) but who seems excellent. Joe is waiting to see what his summer sport will be...we think it will be surfing or possibly BMX. The only downside is that he has to wear a uniform (where Jacob doesn't) which is a polo shirt, shorts (!!!) and black lace up shoes (a real big NO no for Joe!). He seems well settled but for the first week had a real problem understanding what the other kids were saying... but he'll tune in soon!

Jake is at Spotswood Primary School. We sent him there so that from 2 Jan the boys would be very close to each other, making drop-offs easier! Jake doesn't have to wear uniform which he thinks is real cool... and on the very first day he wandered out bare-footed...a real Kiwi kid! He also endeared himself to his new class mates the first day when they had a running race and Jake was seen to be a really fast runner.

They are well settled and we just now need to get a home of some sort to give them a firmer base. It's not ideal being in the motel, although we have a separate room with two bedrooms and a lounge/diner.

Gabs is in nursery (called "kindy") four afternoons per week and one morning and she seems to be pretty happy. In fact, I'm really proud of how well they have settled into New Zealand and school.

We think we have now found a family car...a Chrysler Voyager which hopefully we will pick up very soon. We had hired a car for a few days and then a friend of the motel owner just turned up and lent us a car for a week. Alex had stopped to talk to them about their people carrier in a supermarket car park, they knew Carla, the owner of the motel, and - hey presto - they lent us their old car...that seems to be the Kiwi way... they are remarkably friendly and sincere. Being Brits we are a little suspicious of this over friendliness but it really is genuine and so nice to find. They want to talk to you and take an interest in what you have to say and also have/make the time to talk!

The next thing we need to do is find a more permanent place to live. Still not sure whether we are going to rent or buy...the market appears to be very buoyant and prices are still rising so we are a little nervous of renting, but then we are not sure about where to buy and whether we are getting good value. We know that any place we buy now will not be the final home we are looking for so that makes things a little easier. At the moment we are thinking that if we buy it will be in/nearly in the city so that we can more easily rent it out if that is the route that we decide to go...or it will be more easily sold if we decide on that route...so watch this space! The problem with being indecisive is we are not sure what to do!

We are off to Rotorua next weekend to have some hot mud baths and to show the boys that Dad's 'wind' problems are nothing compared to Mother Nature's! Apparently it is sometimes known as Rotavegas, as it is meant to be a bit tacky, but hey we can do tacky with the best of them. Hopefully, the kids and us will find it different and interesting and that we can get into some nice hot, natural spas.

We have met some English people who had trouble tracking their furniture container down and when it arrived virtually everything is either damaged or broken...hopefully the same fate will not befall us. They used Allied Pickfords and the state of some of the wrapping and packaging was appalling particularly when compared to the lengths that PSS went to with our stuff, so we are holding our breath!

We have the local newspaper coming to interview us next week about how we got here etc and possibly the local radio as well. Self- promotion very necessary here! I have not yet fully started work but will do so shortly. We are just taking on a telesales person to help make appointments for me so we should be ready to roll soon. It will be good to get back to work (see mentally unbalanced me!) and earn some money! That is probably all I have to say just now but more will follow shortly. Hope you are all OK and pls don't feel you can't write to us on e-mail...because you can.

Later guys and gals

Mike, Alex, Joe, Jake, Gabs

Reflection:

Mike:

It is interesting to see that we were worried about whether to buy or rent a house when we first arrived... we are totally clear about it now: rent first, as you really do not know where you should live in your new city and, ultimately, if you are looking at New Zealand as your long-term home (as you should), then why rush? We know (as a rule of thumb) that those who buy within three months of arriving will sell within twelve months, as they simply have not got it right. With real estate agent fees running at between 4% and 5% of the sale price (and you pay for the marketing separately) you are more likely to save money by renting.

We also now know that you can ask for a flexible rental agreement, rather then locking in for six months or more. You will not be offered this but it does exist. Basically, a flexible lease means that you only need to give three weeks' notice to leave and the landlord must give at least six weeks' notice for you to leave.

It may be that you need to negotiate on this matter – perhaps a bigger bond – but you should always ask, as you absolutely need flexibility above all else and the worst case is that they say "no". But you should aim to get a flexible lease if at all possible!

I remember that we were quite pleased that we had the kids into a routine quickly and having them into school, building friendships, was the right thing to do!

Alex:

Looking back it is amazing that Henrietta "the lady on the plane" has become such an amazing friend to us and has stayed in contact with us from that moment onward. Mike stays with her when working in Auckland and she likes to be known, when Mike is there, as Wife Number One, which of course she is not!

She is very much the "true"" Kiwi and always makes us welcome, whether in Auckland or at her beach bach up near Matakana, north of Auckland.

The missing bags *– there is Mike worrying about passwords and bank accounts, but for me I was just* so tired all I wanted was my wash bag and to sleep! I know my priorities were right!

Our internal flight – looking back now I chuckle as to what a sight we must have been, clambering on, wet and loaded down with bags and kids and probably smelling a little ripe – and we now look to see if we can "spot the new migrant" when we travel down from Auckland!

The new boss – again on reflection and looking at the people we have and do now work with, I should have been more attuned to the person, as I don't believe he even coughed up for a coffee that first morning!

Getting around town – initially I used to smile at the idea that New Plymouth was hard to get around but five years on, if I go into town I make sure that I get everything done that needs to be done and really do not like travelling backwards and forwards across town (and hey, honestly it's not that bad at all) and so feel very much a "local" now!

Our GP – you'll remember that he lent us his old car. Well, interestingly, I was speaking to his wife recently and the loan of the car came up and she said how embarrassed she'd felt having to ask for it back. That blows me away, given the tragic nature of their need to have it back (a family member was dying), but again I think it is very reflective of the Kiwi nature.

LETTER 2 HOME - EARLY DECEMBER 2003.

'Here's a very big Hi and G'DAY from a currently brilliantly sunny and breezy New Plymouth.

We hope all recipients of this letter are in good health and bearing up under the dark, cold onset of winter. Thank goodness summer is on its way...hehehehe!!!

So, the saga continues and again so much appears to have happened it's hard to know where to start and, for once, I will try and be a bit orderly in the thoughts. Right, that's over so follow the following as best you can!

By the way, for all you staunch Poms, listen up. When Wales gave the All Blacks a rough time all was a-wailing and a-gnashing. A week later when it happened to England, they turned all smug and started talking about how they wouldn't relish meeting France in the final...I have put them in their places (so should be back in the UK in time for Christmas!) but could foresee us losing to France if we play as we did in the first half against Wales. Mind you I don't think the Kiwis are that certain to beat the Wallabies, so could be some interesting discussions on Monday (by which time I will not have finished this letter so more comment later). Suffice to say, I'm keeping my end up...and enjoying the rugby!

Right. Where to start? I suppose with the news that we have escaped the motel and are now living in the country, but it's literally ten mins drive from city centre, twelve mins to Joe's school and fifteen to Jake's. The locals think we are too far out and had expected us to change the kids' schools "rather than drive right across town". We are still a bit flummoxed by this 'attitude' about travelling...it really is no distance at all.

The house is really nice and very light and airy with an awesome view of our mountain, and on the drive in to the schools you get a great view of the ocean and then drive alongside it for a mile or so...great start to any day!

There are four bedrooms and the kids' rooms are side-by-side with a raised bedroom/platform between and joining the two of them...quite fun, and Jake sleeps up there at the moment. The fourth bedroom is off the integral garage with its own loo and shower and basin. We have a kitchen/dining area and casual lounge on one level with a great wood-burner and then, off that, down some steps in one direction, is a more 'formal' lounge and in t'other direction a laundry area and garage.

All the bedrooms have French windows, which open onto a patio area and the dining area opens onto decking. The kitchen has huge windows which open on a small pretty courtyard with a small fountain... very restful to hear the fountain whilst cooking. The main living area is full of glass, so is very spacious and light and full of sunshine. We also get staggering views of the snow-covered mountain and great views of the surrounding countryside...very restful when we are at home!

Breaking News...New Zealand is officially in mourning as All Blacks do not make the final. England having done the job last night means that all the s**t I took from the Kiwis at the office on Friday is now firmly being pushed back! Looking forward to the final, as there will be no split loyalties now, although already today found a Kiwi who will support the Wallabies next week. Shameful, I know, but what can you do with these old colonies?!

The grounds run to about five acres and at present there are two cows and two calves in permanent residence and a bull on loan...it's that time of year here! They are fine, although Jake had a panic crossing a paddock where the cows were when the bull turned and stared at him. I bravely picked up a piece of wood and saved him. Actually the bull is not ferocious at all but will be cross if you get between him and his cows! I have had to round up one of the calves twice now: one Saturday morning at about

6.15, I'd had enough of one of the cows bellowing so went out and told it to shut the f up...that got five cattle looking at me as if to say "oh yeah? And what'll you do if we don't?!"

I realised she was shouting because the calf had escaped the electrified fencing and couldn't get back in, so I rounded him up and put him back with mum.

I then had the bull snorting at me so I had to decide whether to run for it or to re-set the fence...I chose the latter option. Me and the bull have an understanding. Last nite the same calf had escaped again and so had to round him up again...one more time and he'll end up in the freezer!

We also have three chooks, which we feed on the scraps from the kitchen, along with a little chicken feed, and they give us an egg a day (or, at the w/end, three in one go). We have Jake responsible for feeding the chooks and gathering the eggs and he is getting quite good at it.

We also have a resident cat that we feed but who mainly stays outside. The cat has been in disgrace as he attacked Gabs and Jake the first day we were there. We were told to give it a good kicking by the owners and indeed must confess that the next time it had a go at one of us it did get a kick...it is now our friend and knows not to have a go at us. It has also managed to catch and kill a rat but thankfully not bring it into the house! We did find a dead mouse in the garage on Sunday and Alex had a complete abdab, so I made her pick it up in a dustpan and throw it into the bush. This was accompanied by much screaming and screeching and hopping from foot to foot! Joe is responsible for feeding the cat when he remembers.

We are not on mains water at the house. All our water comes from the rain running off the roof and being stored in an 80,000 litre concrete tank. It shouldn't run out but in high summer we will need to be a little more cautious with our usage. They do say it is just the best water to drink and I think they are probably correct.

Forgot to say that we also have an area of bush (that's woods to you Poms) which has a natural spring stream running through it, so perfect for dam-building, and also a great rope swing. The rope is reported to have been used on the set of Tom Cruise's recent film *The Last Samurai!*

So, we have a rule that, as we can't see the bush, the boys take a whistle with them, so if there is a problem they can whistle. Similarly, we have one for when we want them back.

We have now heard that our container is here and should be in New Plymouth today/tomorrow and should be delivered on Thursday.

We had a small panic, as we found that P&O no longer come into NP Port altho we had been told they did. We then heard that the ship had been to Auckland and was on its way to Napier. Some Poms we know had their container go to Napier and get itself lost for some time and then they found all (yes nearly every single thing) was damaged.

Panic button was pushed on hearing the news that Napier might be involved again and we got the people here in New Zealand to sort it pronto and they now know where it is and when it should get to NP. We have now been through MAF (Agric/fisheries) and Customs and it can be delivered once here. That means that the people we are renting from can come and get their stuff and we can then pay less rent! It will be good to get our stuff as it will help us be more settled. We spent a fortune on Saturday getting fridge, freezer, washing machine, Hoover, iron, food processor etc. Thankfully it will all be delivered today (Monday).

Right what else...? Both Alex and I are mobile. Alex has a Chrysler Voyager on which we have added a personalised plate...so simple here. You can have what ever you want up to six characters as long as no-one else has it! She now has "ALECKA" as her number plate! We got the car as it is a seven-seater and thought that would stop the kids bitching on long journeys...They now argue about who is going to sit where - and that includes Gabs!

It is better, space-wise, than a normal car, though, and drives really well, with loads of space. It's the extended wheel base model so loads of luggage room, too. We have had a couple of problems with it, the latest yesterday when the immobiliser set itself and we could not find how to unset the damn thing. Managed to get the guys out who we bought it from... yep they came out on a Sunday afternoon! It's now in hospital, but should be released later today.

They are a couple of really laid back characters - in fact, one used to be a champion surfer! They are really chilled out here: when you want to try a car you just get the keys and off you go. You can even get to keep it over the weekend no sweat - just so unlike the UK! They even lent us a car before we even bought one from them, so we could hardly refuse when they found this model and had it shipped to NP for us.

I looked quite hard for a car and was waiting to see a Subaru Impreza STI which they were importing from Japan (where most of their vehicles are sourced)... boy talk about s**t off a shovel. When the turbo cuts in, you just get pinned into the seat. Alex hated it and I loved it for its awesome power and stickability but decided caution was better part of valour, as can't afford to lose licence - and I would have in that car... you couldn't resist pushing that throttle pedal down!

I then looked at a Subaru Legacy B4, which has the same power output from twin turbos as the Impreza but is a much more drivable car and much more flexible - the turbos still kick in but on a more gradual basis, so I can go quickly when I have/want to without being too obvious. It is also pretty spacious, so if we go out in it with the kids there is plenty of room...seemingly more that I had in the Passat!

We have been out of the region since we have been here, on a trip to Rotorua to see Mother Nature at work. The boys were amazed that they could find steam coming out of the ground and bubbling mud just in the local park!! They were also amazed that something could smell worse than their dad!

We went up a smallish mountain in a cable car and then came down on wheeled luges. Even Gabs went on with me, and then with Alex, and screamed with sheer pleasure all the way down. The boys loved it. You could go down one of three tracks and at the bottom get on a chair lift back to the top - we had loads of rides down! You then had to take the cable car back down to the very bottom. Bloody good fun.

Jake managed to get on a one-hr horse-riding safari. He'd been wanting to ride a horse ever since we got here...no idea where that came from! He's since been on a two-hr ride and last weekend had his first riding lesson. It hurts his bottom when the horse trots... needs to get into the correct rhythm, just like his mother!

Joe and I went on a quad bike safari for 1.5 hrs, up mountains and down dales and through woods etc. Even came across a completely flat paddock at the top of the mountain about one mile long, where we were able to race against others on the safari - one way up the paddock, Joe was throttle man and, on way back, I was - awesome fun! Joe looking forward to getting his motor cross bike from the container.

We also went to a village which does everything from cooking to bathing from the hot water running through it. The cooking pot is vast and the water is on a constant boil. They also have "ovens" in the ground - put your stuff in and two hrs later it is perfectly cooked...again, amazing. They have to fill the baths first thing in the morning so they are cool enough to get in at night!

We went down to the lake at Rotorua and you stand in the water and it is reasonably cool...wriggle your toes into the sand and – wow - you jump a mile as you come across nearly boiling water. Weird or what. A friend we were with dug a hole on the sandy beach and about three foot down it started to fill with near boiling water...just mind-blowing!

Great trip, but boy does it take a long time to get anywhere in this country. No such thing as a straight road or motorway down below Hamilton, so journeys take quite a while and it is at these time you realise that NP is a bit cut off from the rest of New Zealand, but that gives it a certain charm of its own. If I see the proverbial crow it will get shot!

We went up to Hamilton (not quite the direct route to Rotorua but we needed to get a new key for Alex's car), so Alex could see the town and look at the business we nearly purchased. She was shocked by just how busy the town was (and that was after just three weeks in NP!) Hamilton is a University City, so has a large transient population and it was much busier and more bustling than NP. Al is a small town girl now!

We went and saw the shop and the owner. He remembered me but also recognised Alex from photos. Al was impressed with the shop and the layout but I think we are both pleased that we didn't manage to buy it, as she was not happy with the town at all. We spent some time and money there getting sleeping bags etc so he made some money from us. I was pleased Alex and the kids had seen it, as that chapter can now be firmly closed.

We, meaning me, have had a small health scare. As part of signing on with a doctor they wanted some blood tests done on me due to past kidney stones. The tests showed up fine for the kidney but not for glucose in blood. So more tests...still not good. So more tests where I fasted for twelve hrs and then had blood taken and then drank a very sweet drink and had blood taken one and two hrs later. The idea was to see the blood glucose levels rise and fall in a relatively smooth graph: mine spiked up over normal and then fell back real quick so no smooth graph, but body just about coping, but doctor concerned that I am possibly showing pre-diabetic tendencies so diet needs a slight tweak and the old exercise routine needs to be upped! All just about OK now but it was a worry for a while!

The boys are well settled in school and seem to be doing OK, although Joe has been in a little trouble for not doing as he is told. Might have to have a little chat with his teacher. His work seems OK and he has chosen, as his Wednesday afternoon activity, to do surfing. Alex and he had a lesson with a well renowned teacher t'other weekend and so we now need to find a board for the family but that is proving difficult. Might have one soon, then we can all get down to the beach for some serious fun...or is that bruising!

He has also done very well at athletics and we are told by his teacher that, thanks to his efforts, his school house has done the best ever in competition, so he is well-chuffed.

Little Jake is doing really well and is now in the top group for behaviour and doing work on time, neatly and correctly, and he is the fastest runner in the class so is quite popular. He seems to be struggling with his hearing and eyesight a bit, so that all has to be sorted very soon, but he is still a very happy soul and everyone who has met him seems to think so also. He has also taken up touch rugby and seems to be enjoying that. He sticks the ball under his arm and runs really quickly. Whether this will convert to full rugby in winter, we will wait and see.

Our Gabs is growing and is full of energy but (touch wood) is now sleeping through the nights. She is still not talking properly but more words are slowly becoming understandable. She appears really happy but remains bossy and demanding...can't think who she reminds me of though! She loves her brothers massively and one key thing is that she is getting closer to Joe, who has reverted to being a true twelve-year-old most of the time (not like he was in the UK) and they all get on really well.

Alex is rushing around but perhaps not getting anywhere quickly. She tries to get to the gym a couple or three times a week and then goodness knows what, but time seems to fly by for her. She seems well settled and is managing to look for some houses but as yet we have not found one either that we want short-term or for long-term.

The housing market is very much at a peak so the question is, can it be sustained or will buyers simply back off and allow the market to cool for a while? The gov'ment are looking at restricting foreign investment in land and property, so that might take some heat out. So, do we buy now or later? We will buy now if we find the right property but so far we haven't found it and, jeez, they have so many ways that they offer property for sale: tender; tender unless sold previously; auction; auction unless sold previously; expressions of interest; and just for sale at a certain price...bloody minefield, and the agents aren't the most helpful at times, but we shall persevere!

I have also had one game of golf, having found some very old (they had Christopher Columbus written on them!) clubs at the rental property. Had an appalling round on one of the multitude of very nice courses around Taranaki and so want to have another round once the clubs arrive from the UK...now which course to choose next?! So, all you golfers looking for a new course, I have something like seventeen for you to choose from, so book your tickets!

We are still making some small waves in the community with our video diary. So far we have both been interviewed by the local press, Alex has done a radio interview and we might soon be on TV. We have had a private meeting with the mayor, who we'd previously met briefly in London at the Emigrate Fair, and managed to do a couple of pieces to camera. Joe wandered around with the Mayoral Chains on looking very much at home - could it be a career in politics for him...the Mayor's office is a political position here! Right, well that is just about it for now. If you have got to here you have done really well. It would be nice if some of you lazy buggers could let us know what is happening back in the old country at some time.

Further letter will follow in a few weeks, but till then we hope you all stay well and safe and remember - not many shopping days left until Christmas!

All our love

Mike, Alex, Joe, Jake and Gabs

Reflection:

Mike:

Cars – *okay, culture shock time in that most places seem happy to simply let you take a vehicle for a drive by yourselves and may even allow you to have it for a whole weekend!*

Some dealers will even offer you a "free" car whilst you think things over – there are no catches to this (and as Brits you will be suspicious of this, but it is in this type of thing that New Zealand differs so much from the UK: if you get offered a vehicle and it means you can stop spending money on a rental car I suggest you take the offer) other than they will potentially increase the chances of you going back to them to buy.
Also, do not be afraid to negotiate on price and warranties etc., especially if you are looking for two cars.

Most dealers will be able to show what they have on order from Japan, from where most second-hand cars come. Again, nothing to be overly worried about with a Japanese import – it will be low(ish) on mileage and will have been inspected in both Japan and on entry to New Zealand (and they are now very, very hot on checking the mileage!)

Health *– here in New Zealand, you have to pay to visit your GP and it was odd that you could sometimes hear a GP practice advertising on the radio!*

The reason I was asked to attend a medical by the GP we chose (he was the chap who initially lent us his car) was because of my age and so that he could assess what cost there might be from the Cole family on his budget.

The real difference is that the GPs give you time when you see them. When I infrequently go to the GP, Pat and I usually spend ten minutes talking about family, skiing, surfing etc and then finally about why I might be in to see him! The system seems to work well!

Alex:

The shop in Hamilton *– looking back I am now doubly glad that we never took that shop on and entered a business we really did not know – it would have been an act of desperation! Running BritsNZ in a market we know well is hard enough and I really feel that we would have set ourselves up to fail, but at the* *time it seemed the only way. I am thankful we found another way, as it sometimes still brings me out in a cold sweat looking at what we nearly did! Desperation can sometimes make bad decisions look a lot better than they actually are!*

 **LETTER 3 HOME – FEBRUARY 2004**

'Hi and G'day from sunny, warm New Plymouth.

Welcome to the third instalment from the far country with news that we are still in our rental property. It seems some of you must have lost both our postal address and our e-mail address!

Well, what have we in store for this epistle? Yep, it will probably be another case of printing off and sitting comfortably with your favourite tipple or, given the news about your weather, probably a hot toddy. News about us, Christmas, New Year, our trip and other odds and sods...

Firstly though, to anyone we have not yet said it to, a very happy, safe and prosperous New Year to all and we hope that your dreams come true this year. So here we go then...

We decided that it would be fun if I too had a personalised number plate as an early Christmas present, so my car is now officially "MUTLYS", albeit that I do have to explain where that nickname came from, but, hey, it's all good fun.

Alex, bless her, is now contributing to the NZ tax system as it looks like she has been nicked by a speed camera taking the boys to school. It was hidden in a van on the side of the road. I have tried contesting it: they actually called the Voyager a van (which it isn't) and they got the street name wrong but they still want their $80. I have now asked for the photo so we can see who was driving...knowing my luck it will turn out to be me! The photo has now arrived and just shows the rear of the car and not the driver so it is definitely Alex driving so that's that! Not sure I'm very happy with the police taking pictures of my wife's arse mind! I will now have to pay up, although as there is a kid on his bike in the photo I should challenge whether it was the bike that triggered the camera as opposed to the car - that is going a little far even for me. Perhaps I will get the photo printed onto a T-Shirt for her!

The car is turning out to be really useful in not only giving us space for when we are travelling about, but also for when all the seats come out and we use it to house-move a friend. We got so much in the car including a huge leather sofa and chairs and dining table etc...perhaps it is a van after all! Still, it served its purpose and we got it all moved in record time and really easily.

The friends had to change rental properties, as their landlord kept invading the house and grounds without permission and 'ordered' them back from their New Year holiday to cut the grass! They basically made life unbearable so they gave three weeks notice and then had to find somewhere new, which proved more difficult than they expected. Anyway they got somewhere new just in time. They, however, may have to go to a tribunal to get their deposit back as the landlord is saying there is a mark on the DRIVE! There is, but it is very small and definitely not made by their car tyre, which has a much wider profile. So much for wear and tear!

Housing is still a prob here and we have given up looking at the mo as we have bought a piece of land and may well build on it. The plan is that once ours, we will put the land back up for sale whilst we look at building options and if we do not re-sell at a nicely inflated price then we will build. It measures 761 square metres and is flat and cut into a hill so it is raised up above the house in front but has one higher behind. It has a great northerly aspect to get the sun all day (for those shaking/scratching their heads we are in a different hemisphere so north is good!) and fronts on to a little cul-de-sac, so no passing traffic.

We now need to try and decide what style to build. It will almost definitely be a single storey place with a double garage, three beds en-suite and have a study, but it's whether we build it in brick or have a textured finish or build in wood.

We are also looking at pre-built sections that come to the site and simply bolt together. This seems to give a number of options on the design front and can look quite contemporary. The majority of houses are being done in brick so I am inclined to do something slightly different to make it stand out a little, particularly for when we try to sell on. If anyone is interested, try looking at www.lockwoodhomes.co.nz or www.aussiehomes.co.nz.

Going back to photos, we are slowly building a photo album that you guys can access directly from the web. This will stop us sending huge files across the Net, which take ages to send and which clog up your systems. We can hopefully keep adding over time and each time we send a set up we can then let you know by email and you can access them at your leisure.

We have now been formally welcomed to NP/NZ by the mayor who had all new arrivals to a welcome party at which a group of Maoris made us welcome in a traditional manner. This involved walking along a reception line and shaking hands and touching noses, whilst in the background, the group sang songs to ward off evil and to call upon the ancestors to welcome us to New Zealand.

There were then speeches in Maori and a reply by a 'delegate' representing us newcomers. We were then shown a video about Taranaki and NP showing the diversity within the province and then we had tea and wine. All very civilised. The kids also learnt a Maori dance and tried the Haka and we all got a bit happy clappy but it was a really good gesture. The Mayor gave a little speech and the kids got goody bags. Not a bad way to spend a couple of hours!

I have been back to see the Mayor again, as he agreed to sign our passport forms for the kids because they need renewing as of March. We had a good chat about the Council and where it is trying to go and about the weather (see, still a Pom at heart as must talk about the weather!). He's a good old chap and so passionate about NP and Taranaki (which you can see if you go to watch the Tom Cruise movie "The Last Samurai" which was 100% filmed here in Taranaki so don't be fooled into thinking it is Japan!).

Mind you, I got a bit p**sed off with the British High Commission who I had to ring to sort out some queries (like how much they wanted to be paid!) They charged me $19 to talk to them, wouldn't answer any questions until I had paid up by credit card...bloody Gordon Brown raking in back door taxes again! Is there no escape?!

We are now back to just three cows grazing on the land. The bull has had his end away enough and been sent to pastures new and one of the calves has gone elsewhere for fattening prior to the freezer. Its surrogate mum was not pleased and spent four whole days bellowing for the calf and escaping, leading to numerous round-ups either of it or all of them. Poor old girl was quite upset, as you can imagine but what a racket!

They have learnt the sound of the motor mower and now come looking for me if they can when I am cutting the grass, as they love that fresh cut taste!

The chooks are being a complete pain in the eggshell. They have had to have their wings clipped as they were beginning to fly out the compound but even now they manage to escape. One in particular even seems to get out of a closed hutch and must be the Chair of the escape committee... *Chicken Run* in real life!!!

The prob is that when out they lay their eggs where it is hard to find them so we think they are not laying. We are down to one a day so the others must be laying somewhere, only we can't find them just now. The little buggers make so much mess when they scratch around the garden and we always have a double take when we walk up to feed them and they are coming the other way outside the fenced area! This was particularly so the morning after Alex's 40th party when I was not on top form...I actually passed the damned things in the garden and carried on to the hutch when it finally clicked what I'd seen. Luckily, being girls, it is easy to entice them back to their place...no I didnt get a cock out I just offer them sumptuous food!

Jake, with Aunty Les's and M&D's help, has cleared the veggie patch and has now planted some veggies and herbs, albeit a little late in the summer. Still the earth is warm and wet and the weather is likely to stay warm, so hopefully they will grow for him. I have had some prob with my second hand motor mower but that is now sorted and Joe is now giving a hand to cut the lawns, although straight lines appear a prob just now!

I organised a surprise party for Alex's 40th party. Fancy dress, no less, with the theme being cartoon or film characters. Alex thought we were going to a theme night at a restaurant and even when all guests 'ambushed' her in the house she still thought we were going out!

We had a BBQ, which was a first in forty years of living, as it is not really BBQ weather in the UK at just before Christmas, and all went really well. The kids all got together and got the video camera out and made their own Jackass movie, which was very funny to watch the next day. Our landlord came as Zorro and even went to the extreme of shaving off his moustache of fifteen+ years, much to the dismay of his wife...I knew something was different but it took me ages to realise quite what it was...dooowh!!! Thankfully his wife is very happy for him to keep the moustache off.

Well, the weather has turned against us at the mo with very heavy downpours hitting us. In fact, a couple of weeks ago, the winds charged up from the south and it turned so cold for a few days that we, and everyone else were lighting fires in the evening to keep warm...ouch. And it's meant to be summer.

Thankfully the house is well watertight and not prone to flooding, but the bottom of the drive is covered in washed down debris and soil. All the rivers are at full bore and very dangerous. Some poor chap died just down the road from us when he was swept away at the weekend - mind you he had gone tubing on the most powerful river in Taranaki without a life jacket!

The upside is that our water tank is full to overflowing so looks like no probs for us this summer with running out. The Kiwis do say that Feb should be a really good month, but knowing our Pommy luck, this first New Zealand summer will be the worst they have had for ages. Still, it is warm and we can still get out and about.

We had Waitangi Treaty Day yesterday, which is like a Bank Holiday. This is the day that the Maoris signed a Treaty with the Brits to protect them from the Frogs and in return gave up the land to the Crown.

Anyways, we spent the day on the beach and got nicely tanned as it was a scorcher, and then went to tea with the landlord and had a really good time - and were not given our marching orders!

So back to Christmas. We decided that we would try and do all the Christmassy things going on.

We went to the Christmas parade down the main street in town and got absolutely drowned, as it decided to rain cats and dogs as you'd expect. It was still fun watching all the different floats and things in the parade and the kids even managed to blag sweets from people in the parade.

We went to Pukekura Park, which they light up with multi-coloured lights and lasers as well as the fountain in the middle of one of the lakes and a waterfall. They also light up the little rowboats that are available on the big lake and it is really nice to see these floating over the still water in the darkness, all lit up.

We went to a Carols by Candlelight sing-along in the park, which was surprisingly good fun and again once the darkness fell and the park was multi-coloured lit and the candles were glowing it looked spectacular and was very moving. Even the kids got carried away and sang along.

When they went around the crowd (2000 odd) and asked where people came from the Brits gave the biggest shout...of course!

The following weekend we went to a Christmas at the Bowl concert at Brooklands Bowl (really part of the park), which was OK but not as much fun as I had expected. It was organised by a local Classic Hits (hits of the 70s/80s/90s and today) but they didn't play much of the 'modern' Christmas music which we could all have joined in with, but we still had a great laugh. At one point, all the Brits were up bouncing about whilst the Kiwis sat and did nowt. Those Kiwis we pulled up to join in the action said they'd never enjoyed themselves so much, so we can still teach them a thing or two! In fact, we were taken aback by how restrained the Kiwis appeared to be at things like this. Somehow, we did not imagine that would be the case!

Anyway, Christmas Day is definitely different with it being so warm, although it was not a particularly sunny day. We opened pressies in the morning and the boys were happy with what Santa had bought, although he left snowy foot prints through the lounge area.

Then we went down to the beach where it was blowing nearly a gale and the tide was really high so we could not go in the water. So we met up with some friends and went jet-skiing on the local lake and had some champers to celebrate and then back to ours for a good old Christmas nosh-up, although not turkey! Just before eating we had some people come and collect the kayak we had managed to squeeze in our container for a Kiwi guy. It had been made in Wales and was reportedly one of the best ocean kayaks you could get.

Then we had the boys find their big pressies, which they were really pleased with so all in all a really good day. We had a concession in the evening and lit a log fire just to feel a little in touch with the UK!

Boxing Day was spent relaxing and going to the beach and then off for a BBQ, so Christmas definitely different this year.

My sister from Aus arrived on 27/12 and only just made it into NP airport. They say that if you cannot see the top of the 600 ft chimney at the port then planes will not land at NP but will go down to Wanganui a good two hours further south. Luckily, the weather did improve just before they landed so no extra journey for them.

It was lovely to have her and Alan over to visit, although they were reluctant to discuss the rugby World Cup and they found it very cold here having come from thirty-four degrees to just under twenty: lots of fires lit and braziers blazing on the deck.

We took them around the sights and sounds of NP - that took all of 20 mins - and allowed them to relax as well.

We all went up to Rotorua for New Year and went camping. We left NP with the Voyager virtually touching the ground at the back and Alex at last agreeing that perhaps with all our camping gear and the size of our tent perhaps a trailer was a good idea after all.

I had decided to go the long way to Rotorua (from here you might like to look at a map of New Zealand as we are off on our travels!) so we went south to Wanganui, which is quite a largish town on a big river, and then headed north into the mountains and the ski fields at National Park and then turned right and headed out of the ski fields to Lake Taupo and then to Rotorua.

As we were heading down to Wanganui we had a call from the camp site in Rotorua to say it had been raining for three days and did we still want to go... that would not have happened in the UK. As we were on our way we decided to still go and see and if it was too bad just go into a motel.

It managed to rain the whole way to Taupo (some five hours) and as soon as we saw Lake Taupo the sun came out nice and warm. We went through some absolutely stunning scenery on our way which even the rain could not ruin, some spectacular roads, so I had Alex going "don't look Mike, concentrate on the road"...there were some awesome drops away from the side of the road.

Anyway eventually got to Rotorua and found the camp site and it had really dried out well, so camping it was. This is where we found that our Khyam tent is somewhat larger than the standard Kiwi pitch but we just about squeezed it on. We had a good time and had wall-to-wall sunshine.

We took the boys and ourselves (less Alex and Gabs) on a jet boat ride across the lake and did a number of 360 degree spins where we all got soaked, but it was great fun. Then went through a channel into another lake and shot across that to some natural hot mineral pools where we had a good relax in the hot water and then ran along the pier and jumped into the cold lake, which was only cold in places, as you swam through thermals of hot water. It was great fun and we all came back relaxed and exhilarated.

We went into Rotorua on New Year's Eve and went to the fair and listened to the band for a while but it was a bit chilly, after a really hot day, and the kids were really tired so back to campsite for champers and watching the sky light up with fireworks.

We took Les & Al back to Auckland on 2nd January for their flight home and sort of misjudged the time it took but had a bit of luck in not seeing any police and managed to get them there on time. It was lovely seeing them and knowing they had not too far to go to get home. It was also great knowing we did not have to get on a plane for a long journey, as we were at home!

From Auckland we then headed north to Whangarei to stay at the Homestay I had stayed in when I had come over in 2002...this was to be my holiday! We also planned to see some people who had lived in Braintree and who we had met just before they/we left for NZ.

The drive up was great and we stopped a few times for drinks and to take in the views. We got to Whangarei is the late afternoon and found the Homestay with no probs and were blown away with the views, as the sun was out and the bay on which the house looks out was totally still. Alex thought the place was lovely and we had a really pleasant evening with the owners and another guest who was on hols from the UK.

The next day we went out to the beach near Whangarei Heads. Here we found the beautiful white sand that is missing from NP beaches, and also found the Pacific Ocean crashing in onto the beach.

Joe went in to surf and came out after ten mins with the nose of his surfboard broken from crashing nose-first into the beach...he was not quite prepared for the power of the Pacific waves but went back in to have another go, even with a knackered board, and rode a couple of waves. I went in body surfing and had a really great time. I did get picked up by one huge wave which spun me head over heels in a 360 and dumped me on the sand on my chest...sore nipples that night I can tell you! Still, all good fun.

We walked the beach and climbed a huge sand dune, or, rather, ran up as the sand was so hot, and looked over at other beaches which stretched for miles and miles with really no one else on them. It is an awesome place and very spiritual (no other word for it!).

We then went into Whangarei and sat by the yacht basin and had lunch - very relaxing - and then went and found Tony and Helen.

They have a really great house perched on the side of a hill with superb views of bush and town and seem really settled and happy. Their kids appear to be enjoying the whole experience and are enjoying school etc and Tony seems to be working with a great group of people, so all looking good for them.

To get to their house you have to take a leap of faith as you seem to drive off the side of the hill...the drive down is really steep, in fact so steep that they could not get their container down to the house, so the removals guys carried it down piece by piece. We had a really nice BBQ with them, although at one time Tony managed to set fire to the whole thing and looked like he was going to set the house alight too.

Nothing dramatic about BBQs, you might think, but then this is NZ!

From Whangarei we went up to Russell on the Bay of Islands. It is a really nice, quaint little town, which we reached by taking a small car ferry across the bay. It looks out onto a stunning bay and you cannot quite see the open ocean and the waters are really calm. You can sit and have a beer, and a stone's throw away is the little harbour with the ferries and boats coming in and out and the kids diving in to the water from the pier.

There was a floating platform to swim out to and jump in and out from. I had to go and do that with the boys and the water was really refreshing. A superb setting and just beautiful.

We had a very nice campsite to stay on and managed to cause quite a stir putting the tent up...luckily we had a standard pitch, plus an area where you would normally park a boat and even then only just managed to get it on the pitch. No one had seen a tent like it or as big and we had people queuing up to have a look see how it all worked and what space we had inside.

We also spotted some Kiwis wearing West Ham footy shirts so sent Joe over to introduce himself as Joe Cole. It was hilarious watching these guys' faces as they were unsure of what to do/say and we had a good laugh with them. One of them was a sad man as he supported Arsenal, but then someone has to I suppose!

We managed to bump into a real estate agent from NP who we knew. He spotted the tent which he'd seen on the Net and realised it was us, so we passed the time of day with him. His comment was that it had taken him forty years to find this area and this campsite and here we were after twelve weeks!!

We really enjoyed our time up in the Bay of Islands, but it is a place where you need a boat. We had a great time on a beach we had fun doing lots of body surfing and playing silly buggers whilst Gabs slept and Alex read her book.

We headed south from the Bay back towards Auckland planning to stop near a place called Warkworth to see some people we had met on the flight over and who had a beach-side bach (a Kiwi beach house). We managed to book ourselves into a campsite in a place called Waiwera Hot Springs, in what is known as a wooden tent. Basically it is a wooden hut with a sliding glass door to get in by and a window at the back. There was a double bed with a bunk above on one side and on t'other there were two single bunks. It was really quite neat and worked really well and was so simple.

We met up with Hen and her daughter, Emma, and had a cuppa and were persuaded to go back out for a full day (so that put paid to our spending time in

Auckland...probably a blessing, given how warm it was. It was such a stunning location that it didn't take much persuasion!

We spent one day at the Hot Springs Water Park. Now, it just is really strange to climb on one of those water park giant slides and sit in really warm water and then hit a pool at the end which is really warm too. There were loads of pools with water at varying degrees of heat and we spent all day in there. We even went out for tea and then came back and sat in the movie pool...yep they had a really hot pool you could sit comfortably in and watch a movie on a big screen. The boys watched bits and pieces but spent most of the time going on all the slide rides. We eventually left there at about 9.45 in the evening. It was a superb day!

The next day we went out to Hen & M's place, driving through vineyards and stunning countryside. We went out in their boat (yep even Alex in a boat, and Gabs just totally loved it) to see some of the islands and the coast and then spent the afternoon being towed in the donuts and being thrown off and swimming about.

In the early evening Joe and Jake tried some fishing from the shore. We had a problem with one of the reels that kept jamming, so I was walking out with the rod, dropping the line and walking back so Jake could wind it in!

I then thought it would be neat to take it out using a kayak they had. So, after Joe had finished in it (yes, the kid who would not be seen dead in a kayak in the UK was now really enjoying it) I went over to get in and managed to end up on my bum in the water, much to everyone's delight, including a couple out for an evening stroll who witnessed the whole thing but who luckily did not have a video camera. I eventually got in and dragged the line out but we had no luck in catching our tea.

We had a truly great day with Hen and M and their hospitality was awesome and much appreciated.

From Waiwera it was time to head home. This meant going through Auckland from north to south using one of the very few motorways in NZ. We timed it so that the 'rush' hour had passed and managed to get right through and out t'other side within no more than twenty-five mins. Try that in any major city in the UK/Europe. You actually have to go over the harbour bridge, so the whole city is laid out before you and you also go within spitting distance of the awesome Sky Tower, so you really are going through the heart of the city and yet it seems so easy to get through, although there are huge numbers of Kiwis who would disagree with that notion!

It was a very long drive home taking the best part of seven plus hours, as there is so little motorway and the speed limit, even on the motorways/dual carriageways, is limited to 100kph, so everything takes time. The upside is that you do go through some lovely scenery, but it is just so slow.

It was great to get through the Awakino Gorge and over Mt Messenger and to see our mountain in the distance, as you know you are not far from home. The saving grace about all this travel is the portable DVD the outlaws gave to the kids just before we left, as this keeps them from thinking about how long they have been travelling. You do still need to stop every so often and they will still argue about which movie to watch next but nowhere near the aggro if we didn't have it. Well done, Grandparents, gold star stuff!

News from the UK at the mo is a bit grim. Alex may need to head home, as her half-brother has been in Intensive Care with what appears to be near-terminal liver failure. He has been moved to a high dependency unit and there is even talk of him coming out next week, which will be amazing! He has been poorly for some time, but this has come as an unwelcome reminder about just how far away we are from the UK. Unfortunately Al's mum is now in hospital with a flare up of diverticulitis bought on by the stress of it all. Dad and Bill do not get on with each other, which leaves Gina in the middle of it all. Gina has some college exams that she needs to concentrate on, so is not a happy bunny as you can imagine. We are so helpless over here and obviously can only ring and email to find out what is happening and make sure there are flights available if it comes to that.

In addition, we have been told that my Uncle George, my Dad's brother, is very poorly too. He must be in his nineties and so has had a good innings and in reality we have never been that close, but it is nearly the last link to my dad so is a little sad. But, again, there really is nowt I can do from here. So many people I have been close to seem to go in Feb. It's not my favourite month that is for sure!

Alex and Jacob have roped themselves into being extras in the Taranaki Searchlight Tattoo, which happens over a couple of nights in a couple of weeks' time. They are being Russian soldiers fighting the French to the sound of the 1812 Overture with guns and cannons and noise. Joe, Gabs and I will go and watch and I will have to take the video camera and hope for the best that I can capture some of it and some of them.

There is now talk of doing something(s) with the Operatic Society, so the whole family might end up treading the boards. As long as I can mime in time to the record the singing won't be a problem!

We have now 'finished' our video diary and it is now all being edited and made ready for publication in March, so we are looking forward to getting our copy to see what is in and what is out. We are still planning to run the video now and then to capture our first year in NZ but it is becoming increasingly difficult to remember to take it with us everywhere. It was great fun to do and hopefully most of you will get a chance to see it somehow or other.

Quite a few people are also asking us about the whole emigration process and they are looking for our advice. As a result we are now working on a website where we can set out a few pointers and give them links to useful websites to look at, both for once they are here and also whilst looking to obtain their visas. Who knows - perhaps we will study the emigration process and start up as Emigration Agents. The website is Alex's baby and she is now getting to grips with it and badgering me to write stuff for it. All will be revealed in due course!

We have also set up a loose 'club' called BritsNZ with the aim of getting Brits together now and then to hear how they are getting on and to give each other support and share good experiences, so if someone wants a plumber, say, then someone in the group might be able to recommend a good one.

The last meeting we organised was not well attended. There were a number of other things going on at the time, but it was disappointing. We shall look to do something else in March and see how things go from there. Alex misses the old walk to school and so is missing the mingling with other mums and getting to know people that way. She is now taking Gabs to a playgroup and so hopefully that will help build up an additional group of people to form friendships with. We have been out to supper with our landlords, which was really nice, and they are good people and so hopefully we can meet others through them too.

Well that is probably all the news for now so you can go put kettle on and have a nice cup of char if you have got this far!

We would love to hear back from some of you when you have a moment, either by letter or email. Don't be shy; just write us a line or two so we know how you are and what is happening. Till the next time, you all take care and look forward to spring!

Love to you all

Mike, Alex, Joseph, Jacob and Gabriella

Reflections:

Mike:

Interesting to see just what we managed to do over the first Christmas/summer period and I put a good deal of that down to not having purchased a house – somehow renting simply gives you more freedom and that initially is important. In my opinion, it is very important in those first few months to get out and about locally and more widely in New Zealand and simply absorb differing aspects of your new country and to take an opportunity to see and meet people in different areas.

Getting around is easy and not very stressful and of course the Kiwis are very friendly...I'd strongly suggest planning to take a couple of trips away early on, even just for a weekend, and get to see more of New Zealand.

Christmas is still odd to us with it being warm, but also in the sense that it is not as commercial as the UK and not as "busy". In many ways it appears to be an irritation to the Kiwis as it is stopping them getting on with their summer holiday.

It appears to me (and I really find this odd) that most Kiwis will not take any holiday over the year but save it all for the Christmas/summer holiday period – this means that January in New Zealand as a whole is somewhat like Paris in August!

Alex:

My fortieth *– I feel really "lucky" to have had two birthday parties; one in the UK and the other here in New Zealand in our new rental home in the country. Both parties were great and in New Zealand we all dressed up and it was such fun – the kids loved it. Everyone made an effort and it was a great night. Mind, Mike can be a b*g***, as he led me to believe we were going out somewhere to a fancy dress "do" and I* did not even realise we had somewhat an overflow of food and booze – as Homer would say "D'oh!"

It was also amazing to have so many people come and be so amazingly friendly when we'd not even known them two months before and apart from the people from Mike's office we still see most of them – again Kiwis at their best!

Christmas – it is still strange to have a warmish Christmas but we have a wonderful build-up to it with a Christmas parade through town, carols by candlelight in Pukekura Park and the Party in the Park at Brookland Bowl just before Christmas. I really love the carols – we all sit in the park singing away and, as dusk closes in, everyone lights their candles and it is just beautiful. When we get to sing Silent Night I shed a tear or two and when we do Rudolf the Red Nosed Reindeer, we all have a very good laugh as "ho ho ho" come echoing out of the trees.

Brookland Bowl is a natural amphitheatre and we also go there for concerts (last year, Elton John played his only New Zealand gig there!) and for fireworks. It is a sensational venue and again at Christmas the whole hillside comes alight with candles – brilliant!

It was quite a shock to get a speeding ticket so early on in New Zealand, but that's the way it goes sometimes. Thankfully, when caught on camera you do not lose points...just money! As an aside, I have also been randomly breath-tested about four times since *being here, at least once when taking the kids to school in the morning!*

Final reflection – *I am still unsure of just where Mike got the name BritsNZ and our sweeping arrow but he did, I love it and it works so well for us!*

Mt Taranaki taken across Lake Manganahoe (5 minutes from the city) in Spring 2006 – note the snow line is a lot lower than that through winter!

Mt Ruapehu as seen from half-way up Mt Taranaki. Mt Ruapehu is slap bang in the middle of the North Island and is approx 180 kms as the crow flies – note no towns or industry visible!

This is Ocean Beach near Whangarei, Northland. Totally beautiful and empty in the height of summer.

Ocean Beach continued – the other side of a huge sand dune and even more deserted.

Lake Pukaki as seen whilst driving from Wanaka to Christchurch – July 2008.

The Remarkables as seen from Queenstown and Lake
Wakatipu – July 2008 – awesome skiing, scary roads to
get to the ski fields!

Taranaki barn which has seen slightly better days.

Walking through the alpine forest halfway up Mt Taranaki.

That's what is known as caught being "sheepish" – very hard to get these guys back into a field!

Post boxes in rural Taranaki – all postal deliveries are only to the end of your drive. Post boxes come in all shapes, styles and sizes!

The "Three Sisters" at Tongaporutu, Taranaki coast –
photo by Jack Readhead a very welcome visitor.

Huka Falls, Taupo looking toward the bottom and the
Waikato River below.

Huka Falls – the top end.

Almost under the falls in a jet boat! Back left is Alex's Dad who from five years ago saying he'd never come to NZ has finally arrived...and loving it!

LETTER 4 HOME – 20ᵀᴴ APRIL 2004

'G'day Everyone

Get yourselves that favourite tipple, print this off and take a comfy seat – yep its going to be another book and a half – sorry guys but when I reflect back on what appears to have been a mundane daily existence a multitude of things appear to have happened to report on!

Well, our clocks have gone back and yours have gone forward so we are now an hour closer to you all. Hope spring is proving to be warm and offering you a hint of a lovely summer ahead.

We have had a cold snap with snow appearing on the mountain but the last few days have been glorious with cloudless blue skies and in the high 60s in the day and then cooling at night but not enough at the moment to light the fire. It is very strange to be seeing the leaves falling from the trees as opposed to appearing – yet another first for us to go through. If this is the weather we can expect through our winter then we will be fine, but me thinks not – someone reckons that this will be a particularly bad winter and boy we have already seen/felt the effects of not having central heating. It means no turning a dial and within minutes feeling the heat but rather a streak for warm clothes and then a dash to get the fire lit and then into the bathroom where the heated floor is... aaaahhhh! The other problem is that the design of the house does not lend itself to spreading the accumulated warmth down the corridor to the bedrooms so going to bed is like moving from the oven to the fridge...nipple hardening or something!

Our cows are in calf and babies expected in July/August. Please note ladies that they will simply lie down in the field at the due time and have their calves with no fuss and no noise and apparently no interference needed...in particular, they will not be physically or verbally abusing the bull! The only remaining calf from last year was dispatched to the field in the sky a few weeks ago by the travelling butcher – yep that's right he was slaughtered in the paddock and then sorted and taken away with his offal buried in a hole in the paddock. Alex was determined not to look, as it was happening at 6.30 a.m., but of course the crack of the bolt gun woke us and although she had drawn the curtains she could not resist a peek and then a squeal – what is it with you girls! We actually had some of the calf over Easter and very tasty and tender he was too – all natural as fresh grass and mum's milk only!

Whilst we are still loving this awesome place and I will tell you about what we have seen and where we have been, all is not roses over here just now. The main thing is that we are all in pretty good health at the moment and still very happy to be here – my daily walk along the foreshore and then along the beach looking at the setting sun and then turning to see our awesome mountain means that the spirits do get lifted and the realisation is constant that this is cleaner, fresher and safer than where we were in the UK.

Unfortunately Alex's brother lost his battle with ill health just before Easter. There had been a close call in February and one other time in March but all reports were that he was getting better. He was out of hospital and with some warmer weather had returned to his boat on the canal/river at Berko. He died peacefully in his sleep on his boat, which was exactly as he would have wanted and that was some comfort. Alex had said a special goodbye before we left the UK and had managed to swap letters with Bill after the February close call, so did not feel she needed to go back for the funeral – added to which Bill has said he'd not wanted her to make the journey. Alex was so very worried that there would be no-one at the funeral, but in the event some 150+ people turned up to say goodbye and it was clear from the notes and the piece written and read by one friend that he'd been much loved and a giver of much wise council – a very fitting tribute to someone's life, I think, and something that gave Alex great comfort.

Alex wrote a piece from her heart and her cousin Claire read that at the service, which again was a great comfort. We were up at 3.30 a.m. to say goodbye. Originally, much to my concern, she'd planned to go down to the skate park by the beach (Bill was very good on a skateboard!) Thankfully, she decided that the risk was too great and so we sat out on the deck under a massive, cloudless sky with the stars twinkling away with huge clarity, whilst poking up through the trees was a quarter moon which made it seem that it was smiling.

Alex was a sight, and would surely have made Bill chuckle, dressed in her anorak with Joe's beanie hat on. She managed to burn her fingers trying to light her candle but finally we were able to sit and say goodbye in a truly magnificent natural theatre. The candle she was holding blew itself out and that was a moment of sadness which was lightened by her seeing a couple of shooting stars and being able to make her wishes – it was truly moving and we felt very close to Bill at that time. It was a trying time for her with the loss and the worry about her mum who has been very stoic but the words of comfort from people have been very nice and indeed her cousin taped the service so she could hear the readings, which again was really nice. She has coped magnificently!

We also had a major panic in Feb when we had Jacob admitted to hospital as an emergency case. He'd come up in a nasty rash (which didn't change colour under a glass) and was really very poorly, with a high temperature and being sick so Alex took him off to the GP. She took one look and phoned the hospital and had him admitted immediately. Yep, he had all the classic signs of meningitis! I was with a client, actually one of Jake's teachers, when the call came through so I shot up to the hospital where the family was camped waiting for the specialist to do his rounds. We had to go through the whole story a couple of times and then they left him to see what would happen over an hour or so but they kept popping in to take temp and BP.

We agreed that Alex should take Joe and Gabs home and I'd check in with her when we knew what was happening.

We then had another doctor appear who made the logical step to have some blood tests run which of course did not go down well with young Jake but he was very brave and managed to get through the ordeal without being sick (his usual trick when needles are present) nor with too much swearing (gets that from his mother!) and then it was back to waiting for the specialist.

This was not too bad, as Jake was not feeling too bright and snoozed on and off and he had a TV and video in his room and so I was dispatched to get the odd video or 20! He was in his own room, as they wanted him isolated. Eventually the specialist arrived to have a look and check him over. He was unsure of what was wrong, particularly as the blood tests had come back clear, but decided that Jake should stay in overnight and be checked regularly. That meant that I had a night in hospital with him, as he did not want to be by himself – whilst I had a bed it was a pretty uncomfortable night but most uneventful. He was checked on the hour, every hour, and then at about 5.00 a.m. the little chap's temp took a big hike upwards. This meant that we had to stay most of the following day too until they were happy that his temp was pretty much under control – albeit that they could not determine what the rash was or what was causing it. It is amazing just how exhausting it can be sitting doing very little in a hospital!

The main thing was that he did not have meningitis and was soon on the mend. We managed to get him to a kinesiologist who reckoned that his immune system had taken a pounding from a recent HepB jab and that he'd suffered an allergic reaction to horses. Now this WAS an upset, as riding is his new NZ passion and something he was doing regularly and improving every time, but he had to stay away from horses. Suffice to say thankfully he is much, much better now and we will soon let him get back to riding again.

Whilst on Jake, he has done a number of other things since last writing – mind you not sure how many were of the voluntary nature, more like "step forward, Jake"! He was a Russian soldier at the military Tattoo

– originally he'd been down to be a drummer boy leading the troops out to battle (all this to the 1812 Overture) but was much happier when he could have a gun as a soldier. At the end he had to dance around like a Russian and I must say he was very good if a little out of control. Alex was a Russian soldier as well and the whole thing was very well received by a full house – unfortunately it was the next day that he was poorly so the little (although sprouting) chap managed the whole thing obviously feeling proper poorly.

He has also been in a multi-ethnic parade through the centre of town dressed as a roll of film for a friend who has opened a casting agency – looking at the photos he was not a happy bunny!

He has continued to do pretty well at school and won some more certificates for his work, which is really pleasing – he seems to be very happy there. I have a client who teaches Jake on a Thursday and she has remarked how quiet he is (I had to check we were talking about the same kid 'cos that is not the boy I know) so every Thursday as he get out of the car I urge him to be noisy but he never is!

He has also had to contend with his Headmaster dying suddenly during term time – he was a lovely man and all the kids adored him and Jake was into asking questions about death for a while and became a little subdued, but all in all coped well.

Talking of photos I will shortly be trying to change those that are currently on the web page for a new lot – I'll drop you an e-mail once I have got them up.

Now for Joe – well he is growing at an alarming rate. When we left the UK in October he was a size six shoe and today when buying footy boots he was a size nine. He is now taller than his mother and I am having to wear heels to maintain an advantage – it will be stilts soon! He is now raiding my wardrobe for T-shirts and anything else he fancies – thought this only happened on the girl side of the family but still it must mean that I am young and trendy!

He is starting footy on Thursday, which will be a relief, as I think deep down he has missed playing – he always asks his mate, Will, how Gt Notley are getting on. He will be playing for Motorua but unfortunately will need to play down an age group, as there are not enough boys his age to make a team. I'm sure he'll cope with that though...goodness his feet look huge in his boots!

He continues to surf and is beginning to better understand the waves and surf and is learning to sit and watch others either on his board out in the surf or in the sun on the beach. He is also getting the better rides and it is great just to stand in the sea and watch him – still a prob getting him out but I'm sure there are worse probs for a parent with a thirteen yr old than getting them off their surfboard!

He seems to be doing pretty well at school just now with a very good report – much to our amazement – albeit that all the teachers have commented on his homework so he's now under greater pressure from us to get it done and dusted as soon as he gets it. He is still having a problem with understanding exactly what his teachers want, but they are very supportive and he is being urged to ask for clarification. The school seems to suit him and he is always quite happy to get up and get on with it – which is a relief!

He is getting more and more competent on his motorbike and keeps reminding us how many months are left until he can get his initial licence and get on a moped. He has about eighteen months to go, as he can start the driving process from age fifteen over here – daunting isn't it - in theory on his initial licence with either Alex or me in the car (but bizarrely not both) he could drive my Sub B4 with its twin turbos – and they wonder why the death toll is highest amongst youngsters! I think that soon we will look for a little cross country bike ride, hire a trailer and get both Joe and Jake over to wherever and get them involved. They tend to hold these open cross country rides on people's property and the whole family turns up and goes hooning ("charging" in Pommy) around the place – sounds like great fun but can, I am told, be quite dangerous if they go too crazy – you get upwards of a hundred people on these things!

(Breaking news – Alex (the little toe rag) sneaked off and did her NZ driving test theory paper and passed and is now the proud owner of an NZ licence – my turn next!)

He is still, most of the time, being what Alex and I consider a true thirteen yr old, as opposed to trying to be older, and he has a fantastic relationship with Gabs and for the most part with Jake. When he heard about Bill dying he went into the house and gave Alex a big hug – which looked odd, as she seemed so small against him! For that alone we feel lucky to have made it here and yet the Kiwis think he and other Pommy boys his age are so much more grown up than Kiwi boys!!!!

Now for my growing angel Gabs – and growing she is – again you don't really notice until you see something doesn't fit her anymore. We had thought she was on a growth spurt as she was eating the house out but when she walked in wearing a nighty, which used to be below her knees and was now up around her bum we sort of saw the difference!

She absolutely hates being scolded or told off and still tries to rule the roost. She has developed a temper like her mother and tends to fold her arms hunch up her shoulders and stomp off round the house slamming doors. She had one of these little strops when we were away recently and it was hilarious watching her trying to get the bedroom door to slam –

she had three goes at it! Mind you once the strop's over she comes for a hug and says her immortal "you're all mine" – bless how can you stay cross with her!

She is full of life and, contrary to the above, is generally a very happy little chapess - mind you, as her father, alarm bells are ringing loud. When we'd been away (more later) she'd not walk more that half a mile in the country without wanting to be carried but when we were in Auckland at the shops she never once asked – oh owww a shopper on my hands!

She still goes to kindy each weekday afternoon, apart from Wednesday when she goes to Bubbles nursery. There, she has just moved up a class and is getting some active teaching input. In addition she goes to mother and toddlers each Friday with Alex. She seems to love all these things and joins in all the singing and dancing and always brings some art back with her. She is now beginning to draw shapes – I particularly like the stick thin drawing that she insists is her dad!

She loves playing howls (that is "dogs" in English) with the boys and me and I think would love a dog of her own. She has marvellous conversations with her friends on the play phone and often with Baba (her granddad) who she keeps asking when he's coming to see her and whom she always refers to when anything needs mending!

She is a joy to have and is doing well at keeping beds dry at night although occasionally she doesn't quite make it, which means that Alex and I get this squirming monster trying to take over our bed – strangely I have the feeling that she and her mother have done a deal, because even though we now have a queen-sized bed, it is still me who is left gripping the edge of the bed with one buttock!

Now for Alex – well apart from the upset over Bill she has been on the go a lot. She has been involved in The Tattoo which was a tremendous effort and which she seemed to enjoy immensely. Again, I think the fact she had a gun to fire had something to do with it although it was slightly disconcerting being used as her ammunition pouch – if you know what I mean!

She has been trying to get fit down at the gym and with some running and speed walking on the foreshore which is tremendous fun when the sun is shining and the sea is rolling in – very invigorating! She had her, me and Gabs doing a 5km walk from the port to Pukekura Park in aid of something but still not sure what – the only problem was some PPP (piss poor planning) which meant having got to the park we had to walk all the way back to the car – another 5kms. Thankfully, it was a lovely day.

She has been helping out our friend, Debbie, who has opened a talent agency with promotional and marketing work so is working sort of part-time. She gets all togged up in T-shirt and cap and stops people in the street and hands out leaflets etc. She has really come out of her shell over here and has taken the approach of "what the hell" which is in line with Kiwi culture. I think the plan is that she will also help out in the office and learn to help enrol people onto the books etc – she has already offered the Voyager as a taxi service to get people to castings!

She continues to organise the BritsNZ club and has successfully organised coffee mornings and a BBQ down on one of the domains by the one of the rivers, much to everyone's enjoyment. She has managed to nag me into helping her finish our BritsNZ web site and we are now trying to figure out how to get the damned thing live – as soon as it is we will let you know so you can all log in to www.britsnz.co.nz and perhaps be inspired to have a go at emigrating!

Which reminds me – we hear that the video diary that we were creating will be ready for general release soon (May) and so we are eagerly awaiting our first viewing. Once it has passed the censor we may arrange for a couple or three copies to be passed around so you can get to see where we are and how absolutely fabulous we look darling! Actually it was really good to do the diary and it will be interesting to see what they have included and who the other contributors were and what they went through. By all accounts, we sent in the most footage at about fourteen hours' worth! Apparently the diaries have been 'judged' by a panel of migration experts and their comments have also been filmed and added – we have been told to have our solicitor ready!

Now for me – well I still love being here and most nights take myself off for a walk along the foreshore past a golf club and then come back along the beach – the absolute ultimate in stress relief particularly at the moment with the weather being so stunning – I get to see the sun fizzle into the sea and turn our mountain a stunning range of colours so that your heart is uplifted and all seems calm and fine.

Unfortunately that just is not so business-wise. It is beyond desperate at the moment. I have written next to no business since I really started working back in November – certainly not enough to sustain the family on. I am seeing people, albeit not that many, as the systems in place are very poor and we keep running into problems. Initially, it was the computer system crashing on a regular basis so my reports kept getting wiped. Then we had problems with the telemarketers. Then we ran out of headed paper, so contacting people was put on hold. Add to all that the fact that I do not have a client base to work with and it is like shovelling s**t up the proverbial hill. I'm not sure either about the principal, as he is not focused on the business (too busy building himself a garage), is negative about most things and is not helpful when I ask questions. Also I have learned that the business is off target and could loose its membership of the franchise!

At the moment every idea I have to market the business and to try and create clients and meetings is met with a negative from the principal – I learnt this week that, contrary to what I had been led to believe earlier, we are able to get out and market the company/business locally without having to clear everything through the central management team – somehow I know that this is not a case of not understanding the English used but rather a none-too-truthful summary of how the franchise works!

I have been actively trying to open up the business market but am running into cultural problems along the lines of "she'll be right mate...no worries" – not far off a similar state of affairs with individuals. All this seems to indicate that I will have to be far more 'aggressive' with people which is not something I'm used to or good at!

All of this has cast me into a bit of a black hole and I'm finding it hard to step out. It took so much effort and concentration just to get here that I'm not yet re-charged enough to face this new battle – but face it I must as we are burning too much capital just now. I have been to see a couple of recruitment people but they appear to be struggling – too restrictive a profile even though it covers management, training and sales – I am also applying for jobs from the local/national papers. All those years in the Insurance Industry are coming home to roost.

In addition I have not been feeling too well of late and think that is just an accumulation of everything!

There are one or two things on the horizon, which may turn things round but they are months away as opposed to weeks – so Mikey is in a bit of despair!

So, what else have I been up to? Not a lot really. Have managed one round of golf since my clubs arrived and didn't play too badly but that was a while ago. Have done a little more cow herding (as has Jake who helped Craig take the cows to another farm to have their pregnancy scans – he helped by riding his quad and herding them in front of him– he loved it!) and have built a solid relationship with one of the chooks who must have been an extra on *Chicken Run* as she is always escaping – daft old bird (not Alex the chook!) can get out but not back in! Have started to train the boys – Joe on grass cutting and Jake on car washing – costing me a fortune.

So let's move away from the depressing old fart above and see what else we have done – perhaps this is a good time to recharge that drink and hunt out the map of New Zealand as I take you on our travels!

We have been to Napier and Hastings on the east coast (Hawkes Bay), up to Whitianga on the Coromandel, over to Auckland and down to Raglan near Hamilton. We have also driven around the mountain – no really we went for a drive around the mountain, which is slightly different to being driven around it by the kids!

Right let's start with Napier/Hastings. We decided to take this trip over a long weekend. There is a peculiar holiday system here where the regions each have a day off to celebrate their state – so we went on Taranaki Day which was a holiday for everyone in Taranaki but no where else in NZ – see "odd"!

We opted to take the boys out of school early and drive north to around Taupo for the night and then across to the east. We were about an hour into the journey and coming up to Awakino Gorge (no fuel, no phones, no mobile signal and no people) when - 'bing' - on goes a warning light on the Voyager. Looking in the book we decide that it's something to do with the alternator and even I'm auto enough to know that meant no charging to battery which in turn means potentially no starting car and the locking of security system and immobiliser.

The car was running smoothly enough but we stopped at Awakino Hotel and Alex jumped out and phoned the Chrysler dealer in Hamilton and explained the situation as we could have diverted to Hamilton. My gut instinct had been not to turn off the engine and after ten mins or so out comes Alex to say she has been advised not to take the car anywhere and not to turn off engine. We therefore turned round and headed back to NP. We managed to get hold of the guys who sold the car to us and they said to bring it straight in – remember this is Friday late p.m. of a long weekend. We managed to get back to NP around 5 p.m.

Of course, once in the garage we had a quick check done and all systems seemed to be being charged although the light was still on. We then turned it off and tried to re-start it – it started straight away and NO warning light – bleeding typical that eh!

Al was far too nervous of the car by then so we unloaded to a loan car and headed home to re-load into my car. So having left NP at 2.30 p.m. we were leaving again at 6 p.m.!

Then, bugger me, at almost the same spot my car dash chimed and on came a warning light – we were very obviously not meant to be taking this trip! I stopped the car and had a good poke around and could see nothing wrong and sort of guessed the cause and knew it wasn't terminal. We opted to push on – and push on I did up and down turning, twisting mountain roads until Alex shouted "stop, stop" – by the time the car stopped Gabs had been sick all over herself and the back of the car and both boys were hanging out the window trying not to copy her.

It was at this point that I nearly threw in (or should that be up) the towel – but then I am not my father's son for nowt and we cleaned everything and carried on and hey presto the warning light goes off – until, that is, we are truly in the middle of nowhere in the pitch dark when on it pops again, by which time I am almost totally blasé about it.

We eventually got to our overnight backpackers' accommodation on the southern tip of Lake Taupo at Turangi at 9.45 p.m. and went for the best-ever tasting Burger King – we were all famished. A journey that should have taken three hours max ended up taking over seven and I had the kids scrunched up in my car. It was just so good to climb into a lovely warm bed and shut my eyes!

The next morning we wound our way up the east side of Lake Taupo, which is huge, and then cut across country toward Napier, driving through spectacular gorges and over rugged and craggy mountains and through stunning woods. We finally came down from the ranges and onto the main east coast highway which was a real disappointment, as the land and scenery were not at all pleasant on the eye – it was all a bit plain and scrubby and somehow not what we'd expected.

We finally made it into Napier, which is a stunning Art Deco city, which was levelled to the ground by an earthquake in the '30s and then re-built. There are some amazing buildings and a very clear focus on a café society with little tables out on the sidewalk. It was lovely and warm and we had a good wander round.

We then found the local museum, which had a large section about the earthquake and films of what it was actually like and interviews with some of those who survived the actual quake and took us through the re-building process – the whole thing fascinated the boys. In particular a seismograph and its printouts fascinated them. We could go back a couple of weeks and see that there had been a further quake, which was very marked on the paper – in fact there had been a number of small quakes since the beginning of this year!

Talking of quakes, we had one in the day in late March in NP. The building shook a little and the computer screens went all jumpy – it didn't last long and was barely noticeable. No one is quite sure whether it is good to have a series of little quakes as it relieves pressure or whether it's a sign of something big on its way – we are such a young country!

Anyway, Napier has a foreshore walk but nowhere near as awesome as NP's and the actual beach appears man-made and totally shingle and very dangerous to swim off according to the notices – certainly awful for surfing!

We then headed off to Hastings, where we were staying in a cabin on a campsite – it was basic but really quite good and the campsite was really nice.

The key to the campsite was that it was located right next door to a place called Splash Mountain or River or something! So the kids were all geared up for that which we did on the Sunday and although the weather was a bit overcast it was virtually empty... and the water was bleeding freezing – even after you'd been dunked in off the rides. Still there were loads of things to do – train rides, go-karts, motorised jeeps, boat rides and - thankfully - a hot pool. We had a good time and the kids were happy.

We went out to one of the beaches which was about a half hour from Hastings – great sand but one heck of a trek out over unmade roads so a bit exciting, especially as it was getting dark on the way, but still nice to be back at the ocean.

We left there on Monday morning and headed south to Dannervik (or something) and then crossed the ranges to Palmerston North where we had a look around and had lunch. Interesting drive but scenery wasn't stunning – nice but not awesome!

Palmerston North is one of the main towns on the way south to Wellington, particularly from NP, and it was OK but nowt particularly special about it. We then had another 3.5 hours drive to get home, so a long way – I think in total we did about 1100kms but, boy, it was frustrating driving the Subaru at 100 Ks when there was so much go in it but the boys in blue just love to get you – if you get caught at 30ks over the limit they can take your car away from you instantly and then you can lose your licence for up to three months! Just not worth it but when you have big distances to go and wide open roads 100ks is really too slow.

Our next trip was over Easter up to the Coromandel, which is a spit of land to the east of Auckland and is obviously very popular with Aucklanders. We went up with our landlords to stay at their family bach which is right on the beach just north of a town called Whitianga on the east coast...it was situated in a lovely bay with the sand no more than a hundred feet from the door.

We went up there on the Thursday afternoon leaving here at about 2.30 p.m. and, having stopped for wees and tea, finally arrived at 9.45 p.m. – yep it's a long haul and the last hour is really twisty – in fact, on the way back on Tuesday morning Alex was gripping the seat and grab handle saying "did we really drive along here in the pitch dark?!" – it was, to say the least, pretty spectacular. Again it is just so hard to get anywhere quickly but the biggest plus was that we drove through some really lovely country...AND the car was fine! Gabs did the kids' favourite – get going after a break and almost immediately request a wee stop!

We managed to get all the kids organised – Jude is a total control junkie and likes everything and everyone totally organized, which is the opposite to the Cole clan. She drove everyone nuts until she had the p**s taken and then slowed down a bit. Instead of hot cross buns we had pancakes albeit that Jude did make some fresh hot cross buns in her bread maker and they were yummy. These bread makers are amazing and the bread tastes awesome. She made loads of different types and the smell meant you just couldn't say 'no' – we have resisted the temptation to get one for ourselves.

We went for walks up and down very high hills (worse than being at Aunty Jake's!) to do some fishing and for Jude to snorkel for some type of shellfish, which is a Maori/NZ delicacy. Needless to say we didn't catch any fish but Jude got the shellfish for the BBQ. Me, well I managed to slip over twice – once with Gabs in my arms, but we were OK - and the other crossing a mud stream – yep I was straight up in the air, arms and legs whirling away and then landed face first in the mud – Alex was laughing so much she couldn't get the camera out of the bag thank goodness!

We had some really nice beef whilst away which was our little brown cow slaughtered earlier in this letter – he was very tasty! We also had some beautiful fresh fish caught by none other than little Jake who had gone fishing with Craig and Terry (the experienced ones) – he was the only one to catch a fish and it was really tasty. In fact Jake, Joe and I were the only ones to catch fish – we definitely had a lucky rod.

The following day Jake caught a really big snapper, which Craig filleted and 'cooked' in lemon juice ready for the next day – when I say 'cooked' he literally diced the snapper and covered it with lemon juice and put it in the fridge – the next day he made a sort of salsa and added the fish – it was delicious.

We also went down to Hot Water Beach – this is a beach where you can dig holes in the sand and the holes fill with hot water – you can stand in the sea up to your knees and float in and out of hot water and then wriggle your toes and jump a mile as they get scalded by really hot water. Unfortunately we had not timed the tides right and it was too high for us to actually get a hole full of water but we had fun digging holes and we had a scrummy breakfast on the beach in glorious sunshine. Joe and I went in the sea and did some body surfing, which meant we kept getting thrown up on the beach so when we got home I had experienced massive surprisingly rapid enlargement – my pants were just full of sand! The sea was remarkably warm and it was interesting looking for the extra warm areas heated by the sub-sand hot water.

Jude and Craig had invited another couple up, who arrived with a sail boat on a trailer which they had only just acquired, so sailing was on the menu for them. They got on quite well but then ran into some choppy seas and stronger winds and the kids were none too happy. They decided to turn for home but had to battle against winds and then when running into harbour against a strongish tide – their little outboard could hardly made way against it.

They finally got into harbour but then couldn't get hold of us to take the car down – when they eventually did I had to take the Voyager down, as we couldn't find the keys to Terry's car. (Terry was the spitting image of Alex's brother, Bill, so it was a little disquieting, but Al made light of it!). We then found that we couldn't get the boat up onto the trailer – we were bouncing it, wiggling it, reversing the trailer deeper and really struggling. Although there were loads of boaties hanging around waiting to get their boats out not one offered any assistance – gits!

I had to take the car back to try and find Craig to give us a hand. We eventually got the boat on but not before the wind up-mechanism of the centreboard broke and we all got wet – another day, another disaster, another laugh!

We had some good food – cooked by yours truly – some good wine and beer and some good company – sat out on the Monday night with a bonfire on the beach and discussed the stars and put the world to rights.

On Tuesday we went off into Auckland supposedly for a couple of days to take in my birthday – thanks for the cards! – and had an OK time – I also had an appointment to see a recruitment chap recommended to me by an Old Boy and so it all tied in pretty well.

He is supposedly looking for opportunities for me but I've not heard anything for a couple of weeks so will have to chase him up – he was not keen on the idea of me working in Auckland during the week and coming back to NP at weekends so he may be struggling to get me something Taranaki-based.

We found a place making fresh savoury and sweet pancakes, which were really yummy – quite a treat on my birthday – and we had a nice meal out on the Friday evening at the dock where the Americas Cup teams had been based. The kids dragged us up the Sky Tower, which was weird – thoughts of 9/11 came to mind - but also when you got to the part of the floor with a glass window inset so you could look straight down – the sign claimed it was as strong as concrete given the thickness of the glass but your brain wasn't so sure.

It was a clear day and you could see for miles and look down on all the port activity and see the harbour bridge and all the parks etc – Auckland covers a huge area – a bit bigger than Greater London but with only 1m people in it and they think they have traffic problems!

Alex was getting decidedly down and really wanted to be back in NP on the day of Bill's funeral so we cut short the time in Auckland and headed back to NP and stopped overnight in a beach-side village called Raglan on the west coast by Hamilton. It is a lovely, quaint village with an estuary and the open ocean on the doorstep and is full of charm. We managed to get into some backpacker accommodation on the campsite, which was OK and had a nice evening meal in the village but in reality the day was spoiled by the thought of Bill's upcoming funeral. We set off the next morning for NP and we were all pleased to get home.

We had Alex's really great friend, Bridg's, daughter and her two mates to stay for a while – they wanted to try surfing in Taranaki and were on their way to Rotorua and Taupo – one was doing a skydive! It was really nice to see Donna and embarrass her in front of her mates with the "I remember when you were only so high etc" but, boy, has she grown into a really lovely young lady – lovely on the eye and a lovely character – a joy to have her staying, and her friends, James and Steve, were really nice too.

We managed to get them a tiny bit of surfing but the seas were very poor and confused so it wasn't great, but we tried. We did take them for a drive around the mountain though – down to Stratford and then west to Dawson Falls (which is actually up the mountain) which was OK but not really that spectacular and a good five degrees cooler up there than down on the coast. From there, further west to Opunake on the coast, where we had a snack down on the beach whilst Alex and I recced a campsite for next summer and the kids – yes including the older ones - played on the slides and swings.

We then took them up Surf Highway 45 to NP – in fact it was the first time Alex had been out that way so a day of discovery – being a Sunday and not a heavily populated area we did have a small panic getting to Opunake as the fuel gauge was reading empty and by the amount I had to put in to fill it up was definitely running on fumes when we found the garage!

On the Saturday, we had treated the gang to the spectacle of the NP Multi-Ethnic Jamboree which meant a parade through NP and then a show up at the rugby stadium with loads of stalls and food tents with all different foods from all the different races – actually it was quite good and showed the huge diversity of people in NP.

We have also had a young lassie from bonnie Scotland to stay. She has come to NZ in search of work and the opportunity to emigrate here and we had offered her a place to stay initially. She stayed with us for about four weeks in total and is now travelling around, hunting jobs and distant relatives who she knows are here. She is looking for a librarian-type job and has a couple of interviews lined up. Not heard from her for a while so hope all is well with her.

Well, that's not far off the end of the letter. Joe has started playing footy for the school and not Motorua as mentioned earlier. He had an abdab about joining the club, as he knew no one. Bearing in mind he'd only ever played footy with the same guys since age seven, it was not surprising that he found the whole experience unsettling. He's much happier playing for the school with guys he knows and managed to score a hat trick on Saturday and is looking the best player in the team – that's the coach saying that not his proud dad. His all round game has improved and his vision and passing skills are excellent and the other guys really appreciate him being there, which is a huge boost to his confidence. The only prob now is he doesn't like the new boots he's got as they are black and are not cool enough and they are apparently too big – they are a size nine and are a bit big but he will grow into them for sure – he just is growing more all the time.

Jake is about ready to get back into the horse riding although the place he used to go is now closed as they have moved to manage a new farm. He is also real keen to start playing footy but he's been like this before and given up after a couple of goes – he really enjoyed playing touch rugby for the school during the summer so we will prob look for a junior rugby club for him to join – I think at his age they still actually only play touch.

Gabs went swimming with Alex today and apparently is like a fish so maybe we will see if that develops further for her – the main thing is she is healthy (as they all are), growing and beginning to string intelligible words together and loves going to kindy each day – always brings some sort of art work back.

Well folks we both hope that you are all in good health and wealth and pleased that winter is behind you and that the football season is over for another year!

I know most of you are shy about writing back to us but don't be, we will be just so pleased to hear from any and all of you.

Keep well and God bless the lot of you – all our love

Mike, Alex, Joe, Jake & Gabs

Reflections:

Mike:

Losing someone so far away is a very hard thing to deal with but the reality is once they have died (whether you are thirty minutes down the road or in the UK) you are not going to bring them back, so it's just a matter of the time to get back to the UK.

Actually, the worst thing is when they are sick, as you know, without doubt, that you will not be told the whole truth from the outset because "we didn't want to worry you so far away". This is maddeningly the worst thing that can happen, as we have seen far too often that the truth comes out too late and the loved one dies with you still in the air which is too often totally devastating.

Our advice is that as soon as someone is reported ill and in hospital you get on the phone to that hospital, the GP, anyone other than family, to get as unbiased an opinion as possible and if you have any doubt get on a plane!

There is now an insurance policy we recommend which provides the wherewithal for you to get back to the UK, which can be found on our website www.britsnz.co.nz front page, left hand column under the heading "Repatriation Insurance".

This was an incredibly trying time for me, work-wise, as I could just not make the business get up and run and felt that I was not getting the support I needed to make things happen. Was this unfair? On reflection, no, but I am happy to hold my hand up and say I could probably have communicated my concerns and worries better and been more specific in what I felt I needed!

Driving in New Zealand is an experience and whilst there is not much different, there is the famous Kiwi "give way to the right" rule which applies at ALL times. If you are turning left off a road (even into a driveway) and someone wants to turn right into the same place you have to pull over to the left and let them go first. The issue is about making the judgement call as to whether the car behind you is too close and the person turning right will wait so actually you can go...Our advice is to always pull to the left and wait and no one will be surprised to see you do just that, so no major problems in New Zealand, but as I find too often the first few days back in the UK can be "exciting"!

Alex:

When I left the UK I had a feeling I was saying a final goodbye to my lovely brother but it was still a shock to the system and being so newly away from home I did feel the distance tremendously.

Bill also must have known something was going to happen as he told me quite firmly that I was not to come back but to spend the money on the family.

Now we have a thing called Repatriation Insurance. This gets you back to the UK - or your family in the UK to you - in the case of illness, accident or death and if I'd have had that cover then I'd have gone home to the UK as I felt that I should have been there and was very worried whether anyone was going to be turning up for the funeral. As it turned out, there was a huge turnout for a very special man! I still miss him of course but I know he is with me at times.

Jacob and the Searchlight Tattoo – *I do feel guilty at forcing Jacob to perform. At the time I thought he was just trying to get out of doing his part right before the performance but obviously he was very sick, poor lad – sorry Jakey! One thing now is that I totally know the 1812 Overture whenever I hear it!*

It was also very sad to go through losing Jacob's Principal so suddenly – his untimely death shocked the whole community and I can still very vividly remember being at a school cricket match and kids just coming up and hugging him and getting hugged right back. Of course, still being very much the Pom this was a "shock" at first but how natural and heart-warming it was to see a teacher able and willing to provide that level of care for his children – it is definitely an aspect of New Zealand that means a huge amount to me!

Our trip to Napier made me realise that although the distances might be large, the towns in New Zealand pretty much have the same shops on the High Street and from a shopping point of view we could just as easily have been in New Plymouth. Of course, Wellington and Auckland offer something a little bit different but the main provincial towns are very similar. I STILL miss M&S and Tesco just for the choice available – mind you, after five years such a wide range of choice can be a little daunting!

I loved my time living in the countryside – feeding chooks, chasing cows, burying possums and rats. This was a surprise to me and I am excited about moving back out again once we have built our new home!

LETTER 5 HOME – 14TH OCTOBER 2004

'Kia Ora and a very G'Day from us here in NZ!

As you can see, I am in Wellington airport awaiting a connecting flight to Sydney to see my eldest blister. Regrettably this is not a purely social visit as Les' husband died last week, after fighting a losing battle with Motor Neuron Disease – as with all these things the end came far too soon for a brilliant bloke but there was some sense of peace in the fact that he will not suffer any longer.

It was not the news we had wanted but had been prepared for and so far Les appears to be doing really well – of course it is early days and I hope to be able to give her some comfort and a few laughs in the few days I am with her. To my great sadness I had not been able to be with her for Alan's funeral but hope the timing of the trip will be beneficial...and the mother-in-law has just arrived for her six-month stay, so she and Alex can have some time together without that nasty old son-in-law about – at least that's my story!

Good grief and golly gee whizz - we have now left the UK for just over a year although where the time has gone I have no idea – absolutely flown by – seems like only a couple of months ago we were saying our goodbyes and looking forward with excitement and trepidation to our new life – the excitement is still there but the trepidation has gone as we are sure that we have done the right thing.

So much has happened since the last letter that again I'm afraid this might be a lengthy tome – good luck reading it all. Mind, with the evenings closing in you should have lots of time to take it all in.

I do not have a great idea of where to start so will start with me and see where we go from there!

Well I have managed to start taking control of my life by:

- Getting away from my original employer, which was doing neither my health nor head any good.

- Starting to exercise again so I can begin to lose some weight and feel better in general.

The job thing was just never going to work out – looking back I think I probably realised that on meeting the guy at NP airport that first morning. Nothing ever seemed to be what it was meant or said to be and it became increasingly frustrating and demoralising. Yes, sure, the culture is different here and the attitudes to saving and pensions are totally different, but the type of people I was being pointed at (somewhat infrequently) were never going to do serious business. In addition, whenever I tried to do something differently it appeared to have always been tried before to no good effect – there was never any positivity around and over the ten months I was with them it made me seriously depressed. I knew I had the ability but was not getting any support and with the story changing regularly and with a man who did not seem to want to honour his pledges I was really suffering.

It was a shame, as in reality both of them in the office are decent, good people with great senses of humour (normally at the expense of the trophy Pom!!!) but there was no joy in my life for too long, work-wise, and it was having an impact on the family.

I left my employment in September and a great weight was lifted from my shoulders and I immediately felt better – I was now in control of things. Things are still not 100% sorted as things are not being signed off on the separation deal I believe we negotiated and every time I chase I get nowhere – methinks something might be amiss but at the moment I control the inflow of funds to them so at least feel I have a negotiating tool.

Anyway, that chapter has now closed and I have decided that, a year on, our new lives really must begin – no more wishing or asking for stuff from the UK – if it ain't here we don't have it. I really feel that NZ is home and now refer to the UK as the UK as opposed to home. I don't think Alex and Joe are quite at that phase yet but hope they will be one day soon.

So being in charge (or at least with my wife's permission to believe that) I am now determined to get fitter. I think nearly a year of next to bugger all exercise needed to be corrected and the challenge is on to both get fit and to shed the extra weight that being depressed put on me.

Each morning I am out the house at 6.30, down to the beach where I run alongside a golf course, through a campsite and up onto the walkway. Then it's down to the beach for exercises and the run back to the car. It all takes about thirty-five mins (so nowt too extreme...yet) but it is just so invigorating whether it's clear, dull or wet. At the end of the run I can just stand and stretch looking out to sea with the waves breaking and with a feeling of great joy at simply being alive and so fortunate to be in such great surroundings. T'other day the sun jumped over the dunes and danced across the waves in a multitude of colours and the mountain could be seen in all its snow-capped majesty – who couldn't but feel empowered by it all!

Then on Monday, Thursday and Friday evenings it's back again to run further, do more exercises on the beach and get the chill-out factor at the end of the day. On Tuesdays, Gabs is in for swimming lessons so for half an hour or so I plough up and down the pool and then she and I have play time in the kid's pool – she is like a shiny otter doing most of her swimming underwater but progressing all the time.

Work-wise I am now setting up BritsNZ Financial Services to work back into the UK and try and attract business from the good old UK migrant (in particular their pension and investment transfers) once they hit our shores. I have done a fair bit of research and know there is value in this market albeit that the timelines are longish and that it is likely to take me two years(ish) to get the whole thing running smoothly. I will be advertising the service in the Destination New Zealand newspaper and through our website on www.britsnz.co.nz which is in the final (I hope) stages of a restructure and should be up and live really soon – so take a look when you get this letter!

Obviously, it has helped doing the video diary, as the DVD has attracted e-mail traffic already – and we are about to be in the Sunday Times magazine! They are doing a feature on the exodus of Brits and have contacted us to be the NZ side of the story. We have been interviewed over the phone and had a family photo taken by a professional photographer which we understand has resulted in us being on a double page spread. The feature is running on 24/10 so hopefully you will get either this or an e-mail from us to say go buy the Sunday Times that day – we obviously take absolutely no responsibility for any sickness caused over the breakfast table by said photo!

They have said they will include reference to our website in the feature but as we have not seen the piece yet we do not know for sure that is going to happen but if it does that will be a brilliant bit a free advertising!

There are going to be a number of new photos on the website of us and NZ so please do take a chance to have a look if only to see those photos!

Alex is about to take a great role in the 'club' (we use the term loosely) that we started, as it will hopefully enable new arrivals to know about BritsNZ and then look to use my financial services to help them settle.

I have done a deal with a group called Paragon Insurance & Investments Ltd to sort of contract my financial advisor skills to them and to use them as a channel for BritsNZ Financial Services. As they don't really do the investment bit they will hopefully be referring people to me who want/need that type of advice. It is a good deal that we have struck, which gives me access to providers and potential business, whilst allowing me to build my business and have the freedom to pursue my other work avenues – also everything is more on my terms so I feel much more positive about this venture.

We have been talking to Venture Taranaki (a sort of regional business agency) about offering a migration service where we would work in conjunction with local employers who are looking for staff and who would be happy to take a Pom immigrant. The idea will be to help in the interview process, but with our focus being on whether we think the family will make a success of moving down under. There have been a number of couples that have made the move and it has been anything but successful and when you are trying to sell a region any negativity is unwelcome.

Our role will be to make sure that the best possible people are chosen for the job and for settling in NZ. It would mean a number of trips back to the UK to emigration fairs etc, but it is something I am really keen on, as I believe it would suit me/my character down to the ground – so that is another project I am working on and which I can hopefully resolve this year.

Talking of shows, we have just found out that we are going to be sponsored back in March to attend a show and sit on the panel and take questions...Alex is already worried what she's likely to be asked! At the moment we are planning on us all coming back and possibly for about four/six weeks. Once we have the plans in place we will let you all know and then hopefully we can arrange things so we can see as many of you as possible. One word of caution though...**WE ARE <u>NOT</u> TELLING THE KIDS UNTIL**

MUCH NEARER THE TIME SO PLEASE BE VERY CAREFUL WHAT YOU MIGHT SAY IN ANY CONTACT WITH US/THEM...thanks.

It appears we will be in the UK over Easter and for a while after but have yet to decide quite what we will be doing... watch this space!

I am also helping an English friend with sales and marketing on his flooring company. He does wonders on concrete floor with polyurethane screeds and epoxy resins. It is slow at the moment but we are chipping away and know once the first couple of jobs come in we will be away.

We are experiencing the frustration of lack of commitment and communication, which in business is probably not just a Kiwi thing. It will be a great business but we just need those initial jobs. I thought I had landed us one in Auckland, but at the eleventh hour the client changed their minds – the architect we were dealing with was sort of at his wits end but that doesn't help us get the work in...we will keep plugging away!

Finally on the work front, I am also helping out a chap who runs a company called Taranaki Outdoor Adventures and indeed have just been asked to become more involved. He does, obviously, outdoor stuff but also putting together events and team building etc. I have helped on the team building and also on a couple of occasions acted as his chef for twenty or thirty people, which has been great fun – you know how much I love cooking and those were great challenges...and, no, before you think it - no one was carted off in an ambulance!

There are a number of things coming up before Christmas and in the summer so that will be great – both to do something so different and to earn some more money!

Not surprisingly that is just about all I have on the work front!

The NPC Rugby season has just finished here. We (yes the WHOLE family!) became season ticket holders and went to all the home games and enjoyed it a huge amount. The kids got restless at times but seemed to enjoy parts of every game and Alex really got into it big time...and it was just great to go and do something like this as a family. I lost my voice on a couple of occasions from urging on the Taranaki boys. They had a great season and just, just, just missed out on a semi-final place, which was a shame. Jake had a plastic trumpet and bullhorn and used to try and make as much noise as possible and the atmosphere and the people around us were great. The 'Naki mascot is a bull (dooowh, I mean a man dressed up as a bull) and Gabs just loved to run down to the front and squeal and shout for his attention – of course once she had it she invariably went shy!

15 October Corrimal, South Sydney

The sun is out and the sky is clear and - hey - it is warm – somewhat more so than NZ.

Now at my sister's place and of course due to time difference woke on NZ time to find it was four in the morning here! Never mind, been down for a good walk along the beach – which was strange as they have golden sand here as opposed to black sand in NP!

Right so where was I for me...I have been up and down to Auckland a few times which just highlights to me how 'remote' NP is – you are looking at between four and five-and-a-half hours to Auckland depending on how often you push the speed up over the 100 kph mark.

I know now that NP is not where I want the family to be long term and next year Alex and I will start looking to find somewhere north of Auckland. As lovely as NP is with the beach and the mountain my soul is not in the place and I do not want to stay here long term. This is likely to be a problem for/with Joe but a bridge to cross when we get to it.

It also has this quality of being remote and having a small town quality where it seems people know your business – the problem with that is that you sometimes get the feeling of having no privacy (the landlady has on a number of occasions known what we've been doing because it gets reported back) and also that if you upset someone your name is on a blacklist (the concept of the small town never seems to work in one's favour) and hence you feel, at times, that you are walking into a pub where everyone stops talking and looks at you – we are definitely outsiders still – even though we have done a number of things within the community to integrate.

Ever since I came out in November 2002 I have felt a connection with places to the north of Auckland – sort of between Auckland and Whangarei – and that is where we will start to look. The point is that I can do the Financial Services and the flooring from anywhere – the work for Venture Taranaki is different and so may delay a move, but if I can pull that together and do that for, say, a year or so, then I will have a portfolio to offer a similar service to another regional development board.

Now what else...as Alex was working (more later) through the kids last school holiday I thought, after Jake's ninth birthday, I would take them away for a week to give her some peace and to stop me being pulled all over NP by three kids all wanting to do something different.

I took them away to a friend's beach bach near a town called Warkworth – I know, a touch of winter madness setting in! We had a good week doing things together – we went to the glow worm caves at Waitomo on the way north – there is something surreal about sitting in a dark cave looking at a worm's arse which happens to be glowing at you!

We went to a sea life sanctuary at a place called Goat Island (no mother-in-law jokes thank you!) where we saw some stunningly blue coloured fish. We went to the hot springs water park at Waiwera for the day. It was quite cool as days go, but the water was lovely. The boys went off and did all the flume rides (which is an odd sensation – not so much the ride but the fact that you sit in warm water!) and Gabs and I went from pool to pool just swimming and playing. Whilst it was cool when you were out of the water the sky was clear and the sun shone to the extent that we all got burnt – me quite badly. As usual I hadn't thought to pack the sunscreen!

We went into Auckland and saw a movie all together and generally had a good time. It was lovely having the kids to myself and it was the first time we'd been away without Alex – which was novel. Unfortunately the last night in the bach Joe managed to throw up all over the place – a dodgy MacyDs – and both Jake and Gabs fell out of bed – all virtually at the same time!

On the way back to NP we stopped for lunch with the lady who owns the bach and Gabs managed to get some Coke down her throat – quite literally from 9.30 until we got home at about 6 she just did not stop jabbering on – and there I was not so long ago wishing that she would talk more and here she was not stopping – "are we there yet/I'm bored/the boys wont let me see the DVD/I want some more yummies". It was totally exhausting – bless her.

OK that is more than enough about an old codger like me so let's move on to Alex...

Thankfully she has been embracing the work ethic with some gusto leaving me to mind the kids more and do the housework – sucker for punishment, me!

She has been doing some cleaning for our Adventure Lodge owning friends who had a group of about a dozen Japanese engineers staying for six weeks and whose rooms needed cleaning daily – something which Alex is very good at and in which she takes a good deal of pride.

From that stemmed another cleaning job at the Lodge next door, which was for a couple of hours a week – and which she used to get some help occasionally from Joe – for a fee of course!

Both cleaning jobs are now finished, but she enjoyed doing them and it brought in some cash and got her out of the house so a good period for her.

Recently she has been working for the Council. She was on a three-week contract helping to process votes in the local elections. This involved waving a scanning pen across ballot sheets and checking and re-checking the process. It was a fixed fee contract and she was meant to work 9 to 5 but usually finished by lunchtime each day – the NP people were not overly enthused about voting!

Again it allowed her to earn good money and get out of child caring for a while – but the poor girl was knackered – obviously needs more practice! It all went extremely well and Taranaki were the first Council to declare its results and with total accuracy – unlike other areas of the Country. Our favourite Mayor got back in to office so a good result and she made a load more contacts.

It now looks like she may have a job invigilating at the forthcoming school exams – this is, of course, somewhat amusing given Alex's school record but again it is only temporary and doesn't have a major impact on the family, time-wise, and is income. So that will be good again.

Earlier this month the clever old soul managed to run a half marathon in 2hrs 18mins without stopping in pretty warm conditions having never done this before. She was dead proud of herself as I was too – she did brilliantly.

It now looks like she has got herself into a group to train for a marathon in March –the way her body was after a half marathon good help her/us after a full one – hence the group training. I offered to join her but as the first run is for forty mins and as I HATE, HATE, HATE running distances I don't think that is for me! Mind let's see how long the old girl lasts, as training is at 8 a.m. each Saturday morning and she is very much a pillow girl especially on Saturdays!

Alex has also found some casual work at a local private kindy looking after babies – which she loves but which she knows will NOT be happening for her again (another baby that is!) They just ring up when they want her and if she can go then she does the time. It also means that, if need be, when she is working Gabs can go into a separate part of the kindy at a fraction of the normal cost freeing me up to do my thing – like put my feet up and have a snooze...as if I would!

When my sister from the UK was over in July/August she'd set us a challenge. On her 25th wedding anniversary she gone to the Grand Canyon and it was to be their 30th anniversary when they were with us.

So...I made them and Al paddle a kayak over the top of a dam - more than once - and if you look through our web site you should see some of the pics of that event. We then went for an hour's paddle shooting rapids etc and falling out a lot – thank goodness for wet suits...and thanks to Tran at Taranaki Outdoor Adventures. I think that Alex and my sister and her husband enjoyed it – the main thing was that although it looked daunting and at the top of the dam before you head downwards you are definitely thinking, s**t what am I doing? They all did it!

19th October Sydney Airport

Well I am now on my way back to NZ having spent some time with my sister. She is just about hanging in there and I am really proud of the way she has managed to cope with everything and to be able to chat and laugh about Allan – he touched so many people and all of them in such positive ways.

She is organising herself a trip round the world, as she needs some space and time away and she needs to be in the UK for a memorial service that Al's family are organising. So she is off to Thailand for a trek on the elephants to the Golden Triangle (I've told her the elephants will need to go into training to get ready for her – made her laugh and then thump me!), then to the UK, then Barcelona, Rome, Prague, Cyprus, Greek Islands, Madrid, Peru and then to us in NZ for Christmas – she's flying her daughter, her fiancé and son across so we are suddenly having a big gathering for Christmas but that will be great – let's hope for good weather!

Right back to Alex. She has been on the go all the time but for the life of me not able to remember everything she's been doing so no doubt she'll add anything I have forgotten. One thing she has worked hard on is our web site www.britsnz.co.nz. The idea of it is to help people get to NZ by letting them see what we went through and by trying to give people an idea of the things they need to think about and plan for to make their migration successful. It is also going to be a contact point for my Financial Services business. She sorted so much stuff out and decided the form and layout. The whole thing is now live and very nearly as we want it – just a little more tweaking to go and we will be happy with it!

Sunday 31st October 2004

BREAKING NEWS......If you haven't seen us, you have missed us, as we were in the Sunday Times Magazine last week! Some people are still in hospital whilst others had stronger constitutions. I just had an e-mail from an old school friend who reckoned I'd not changed since we left in 1975 – I reckon it must have been your guide dog saying that Jerry!...or you are being bloody rude and saying I looked really old when I was nineteen!

Since last Sunday we have had nearly 10,000 hits on the website and over two dozen e-mails which is great – we now need to help those that need it to get here and those that are coming we need to try and convert into a business opportunity. And here is the photo

Right, that's probably all about Alex...at least until she reads it and adds anything else.

So now to the kids:

Joe – we are now in the final term of his first year at high school and he at long, long last seems to be settling down and not getting into trouble. It has been a hard year for him (and us) so it is with a good touch of wood that we are hoping/praying/beseeching that a corner has been turned.

It seems like he has taken the move the hardest – yet strangely in the UK he was always the most positive about coming here – when we might have been faltering he was always looking forward – obviously the reality of leaving his close circle of friends was worse than he/we imagined it might. A good example was when we came to the start of the footy season – we took him to a local club and he flat refused to even walk onto the pitch getting very upset in the process. We realised that this was to be the first time in his young life that he was going to have to play the game he loved and was very good at without any of the friends he'd grown up with and we realised then just how difficult some things were for him. Thankfully we managed to get him involved in the school team, about which he was far happier, and he had an outstanding season, his level of skill and vision being far greater than his Kiwi team mates – only to be expected when football (soccer here!) is such a minority sport!

He keeps saying that he wants to go back to the UK and his friends but makes no real effort to stay in contact by e-mail, MSN or phone so not sure where he really is on this score. Going back in March will be interesting – we are taking the precaution of being able to bribe him with Disney in California on the way back just in case he starts thinking of not getting on the plane!

As for school...well he's been a nightmare and communication between us and the school has been difficult to say the least. The school principal seems more interested in raising funding than giving the kids a strong framework to work within. It appears that we are still, at times, experiencing this language barrier of both speaking English but things not having the same meaning. He has been skipping lessons, getting endless detentions, being required to go in on his school holidays to help clean up and suffering a teacher's huge anger by claiming she was picking on him as he was a Pom! Unfortunately he also played truant three times – the second time being picked up by the truancy officers in their van. None of this seemed to have any impact on him, as neither did being grounded for a month and without any of his games, TV etc.

At the time, whenever Joe was in trouble, there was always the same kid with him. We spoke to his mother a couple of times and she too was in despair about what to do. Like us they had recently moved up here in the year (she and her husband subsequently parted!) and it appeared that of her six kids he was having the most problems. It looked like they were both leading each other and others astray. Thankfully this kid then did something to totally piss Joe and his best mate off in a major way and they have stopped hanging around each other – since then there has been a marked improvement and hence the wood touching.

As I said he has had a great footy season playing wide right midfield and playing well – just needs that little extra boost of confidence to start encouraging, guiding those around him. They had a good season – they lost two games out of ten in the first half and three out of eight in the second. He also played a couple of times for the school's first team, so a good result.

He is very much looking forward to warmer weather and getting back in the surf – he's had a number of offers from people to go out with them and learn from them and hopefully he will take up those offers. Again he just needs more self-belief, as he is quite a natural on the board – he has a healthy respect for the sea and now just needs to learn more about the wave patterns and sea conditions.

He's now started to play touch with me (and Alex when she's not injured) – in fact last week we had the three Cole boys (Jacob is very good at it as well and will be playing for the school through summer) all out on the pitch playing touch together! Stirring stuff!

Jacob – thankfully, with regard to school, he is the exact opposite to Joe. He has done really well and is in the top group for a number of things. In fact, at the end of last term he'd done so well that the school took him for an afternoon off at the Aquatic Centre!

He can be a little bolshy at times (but then he's learning from an expert – that's Joe not his mother... or is it??) but in general he is well-balanced and usually a happy chap with a ready smile and a good sense of humour. At the moment he's busy writing books and songs and says he's going to form a band when he's older!

He has not done a whole hell of a lot of sport this winter but as we said above will play touch through summer and we hope to get him back horse riding at some stage and also into the water with the boogie board. Joe had him standing up on the surf board when we were away in September being pushed backwards and forward between me and Joe – and he didn't fall off once. He keeps doing his thing on the tramp and Alex and I really must find him somewhere he can go and get into that again.

He did take part in the schools cross country although he was really not well at all – temperature and bad cough – so much so that the teacher almost sent him home. He insisted in running and to his great credit did not come last and tried his very best – we were really proud of him!

He has his moments with his brother (one day Joe will get a real surprise, as Jake will lash out and smack him one). He also has his moments with Gabs – he was recently in big trouble for punching her in the stomach, albeit that she was really winding him up. Unfortunately, with Grandma here he is back to sharing a room with Gabs whereas he'd really like to be on his own!

He seems to have a good group of friends and apparently is popular with all the kids – in fact, his teacher said at a teacher-parent meeting "Ah Jacob – yes, he creates me a problem daily" (of course our hearts sank) "everyone one wants to sit with him and be next to him so I have to try and work out a sort of rota" (heart rates returned to normal!)

Gabs – she (like the other two) is growing at a huge rate and is really beginning to speak much better, longer, intelligible sentences. She has even, much to everyone's amazement, got up in front of kindy, on a stage, to tell them all who she'd dressed up as on dress up day – Barbie! It still amazes us how, with two older brothers, she seems to love and instantly relate to all things girlie – dolls, dressing up, nicking Mum's make up etc – it really must be in the genes.

She now goes to kindy every morning and bounces in quite happily but them becomes quite clingy – so far I have painted at least a dozen masterpieces in an effort to get her to let me go. She now has a kindy mum who she is happy to go with – I now call Meredith 'mum'!

She runs round like a looney and can mince across the room like the best models in the world. She loves looking at books and having stories read to her and is excellent at identifying colours and counting up to ten. She is beginning to write coherent shapes and letters and can identify her 'best' friends. She struggles on some words by not managing to get the first letters right, particularly 'S's – her friend Siani is Hiani!

She can still be totally demanding and when she wants can get everyone running around doing her bidding – anything for some quiet!

When coming down from Warkworth after our break she did not stop speaking the whole way down – all six+ hours of the trip – it was totally exhausting – she didn't sleep once in the car and within twenty mins of being home had driven Alex mad – and to think we used to worry so much about her not speaking – oh, Halcyon days! She obviously feels she has something to catch up on – just hope she's over it before she marries some poor bloke!

She currently goes to swimming lessons every Tuesday afternoon and is becoming a right little otter – almost happier under the water than on it. She is swimming strokes and is showing no fear – won't be long before she will be away on her own!

She is full of mischief and questions but touches your heart each night when she hugs you goodnight and says, "You're all mine"!

Well, we are nearly done – hurraaaaah I hear you shout!

Last weekend we made our first sojourn down to Wellington for the long Bank Holiday. It was a strange journey – winding roads up and down hill as normal until we got to Bulls and turned right and then suddenly we were on dead straight flat roads almost all the way down to the capital. Then as you near Wellington you run right beside the water and then up through a series of gorges.

We actually stayed a little way out from the city in a place called Johnsonville in a nice motel. It took literally ten minutes to get down into the city the next morning. Wellington was the exact opposite to Auckland in that it has a compact centre with all the government buildings on the edge. Loads of good shops – Alex and the kids made some serious shopping hay for the first time in over a year – the shops must have thought Christmas had come early.

We went up on the hill tram, which takes you to one of the high spots in the city. It gave great views out over the harbours and the city and the surrounding hills. Again one of the 'strange' things about NZ cities is the presence of bush almost all the way into the city centre, giving it a much softer look. Still plenty of tall buildings but just a much nicer, greener place.

We managed to get tickets for the NPC Rugby Final, which was at the WestPac stadium in Wellington, and whilst it was interesting to be inside one of NZ's international stadium, the game itself was not exciting and the rugby was poor...we left with five mins still to play. We had opted to go to the game on the train, which wound its rickety way around the cliffs and gorges into the city, stopping right outside the ground – it was a bit of fun and the kids enjoyed it... Gabs managed to fall asleep on the way down to the game, much to everyone's amusement, as the train was packed sardine-style.

On the Sunday we went to do more shopping – never-ending once started – and then took the kids swimming etc – more of a lazy day thing. Then on the Monday we went into the city again and walked around the parliament and government buildings and into the cathedral. Amazingly, there were absolutely no obvious signs of security – no police and no lack of access and we could even have gone on a tour of the parliament but didn't think the kids would cope with that for an hour!

Wellington was really nice and we know we will definitely visit again – perhaps without kids!

One last thing – I will be adding another section to my CV soon, as I have to help our landlord castrate the young bullock currently in residence. Apparently, if you don't, he'll get very aggressive and hump everything in sight. Mind, the thought of popping elastic bands over its cojones made my eyes water and Craig reckons the bullock will walk around on his hind legs for ten mins or so until the numbness really cuts in! Can't wait to help...not...and I will definitely be keeping my legs tightly crossed just in case!

I think that you are probably all up to date now with what has been happening down under. November is about to start, so Christmas is nearly here...so, as a thought, we would like to take this very early opportunity to wish all of you a truly festive, happy time over Christmas and a wonderful, happy, healthy financially secure New Year – and we are looking forward to seeing as many of you as possible in March – more updates when we have some firmer dates.

Take care, keep well and why not drop us a line and let us know how you are and what is happening.

Love to you all,

Mike, Alex, Joe, Jake & Gabs
xxxxxxxxxx

Reflections:

Mike:

It was interesting that at this time I was saying that we would not stay in New Plymouth and I think it fair to say that it was only after our initial trip back to the UK that we returned to see the surf and the mountain and to hear the kids happy to be "home" that we realised that it was a great place to live and actually had everything we needed to give us a full life. We are still here and absolutely loving it!

The first trip back to the UK for the shows was interesting and successful and whilst the kids did enjoy seeing old mates I think they also realised that both they and their friends had all moved on. It did give us a glimpse of what we had left and confirmed to us in many ways that we had done just the right thing. Being at the Emigrate Show and speaking in front of so many people was exhilarating and something I fully enjoyed and still do so today. I often get told by my fellow panellists that I do not "sell" my business very well in the seminars but I see it as a giving of information forum not a selling forum and now find that as I am one of very few Kiwi companies up at the shows and usually the only migrant, we attract people on the basis of "been there and done that" which is pretty powerful for us!

It is also interesting that all the kids have now really integrated themselves into Kiwi life and with Joe nearly finishing school (and yes he has stayed on to the equivalent of A-Levels in the UK) and the other two going through the process, we see them as Kiwi kids.

With about six weeks left, Joe has declared that he is now enjoying school; we will move Jacob away from an all boys school next year, as he doesn't appear to be enjoying himself very much; and Gabs is having a much better start than we remember the boys having in the UK – no SATS tests for her but she is still learning to read, write and do maths along with a host of other things without the stress of being forced to do a test to make the school look good. Why do we Brits allow that to happen? It is so pointless for a seven-year-old to be tested.

Also, and I do get very passionate about this, all the kids have a greater sense of freedom as they are not being schooled in cages as they are in the UK. I was in the UK when Dunblane happened but now having been in New Zealand and seen the greater sense of freedom the kids experience I am staggered that we as parents in the UK believe it is okay to send our kids to a cage each day. It is fundamentally not right and will not stop another incident if someone wants to kick off...and before anyone says that you can't do anything you absolutely can – you just need to start "beating" up your MPs and get them to instigate change. Remember, you put these guys in power and you can change that at the next election – they are working for you and if you do not like something, tell them!

We still have a great relationship with the Paragon guys but our business has moved on year on year. At the core is still financial services, but we are now very much a "one-stop-shop" for all things related to emigrating to New Zealand and have worked non-stop to build relationships with other providers to ensure that the service people get will be at the same level and commitment that they get from us.

As with all new ventures, it has taken a considerable time and effort and certainly in the first two years I did not take a day off. This is not bragging, but simply pointing out what was necessary, and I absolutely could not have done this without Alex as my wife and business partner, nor without the help and support of the kids, who have been magnificent in their support. And to my little Jake, a big thanks for occasionally putting his foot down and making dad stop for a while and come and play – thank you for that, my little man!

Alex:

The second death in the family again highlighted the difficulties of getting to your loved ones in need. Due to costs and timings, when Mike's brother-in-law died he simply could not be there for the funeral. In the end it worked well that he could be with his sister for a while after to give his support, but to me it simply highlights the power of having Repatriation Insurance which pays for you to go in these circumstances.

Mike stepping away from the job was, of course, a huge concern and I was also worried that he had not shared these fears and worries with me earlier, although I admit it would probably have spooked me into wanting to head back to the UK. Thankfully, even though these were very stressful times, just like when we went through the visa process we were never down together and we both, but Mike in particular, kept a very positive outlook on everything. I also recognised that for Mike being truly independent was what he most wanted and, having moved, what did we have to lose by giving it a go? An early "she'll be right" New Zealand attitude for the Coles!

Again, looking back, I feel we did the right thing in joining Paragon. We had been talking to another company but neither of us felt completely right, so took a deep breath and opted to listen to our guts and not take that option and then up pops Paragon – lesson learned to listen to our intuition a bit more!

The initial time working for the Council doing the local election counting was great – it gave me confidence that I was employable and I could make things happen for me. It also got me out and into the community and helped me make a range of friends that I still have today. I must have done okay, as I have been back again to the last election!

I would say that finding part-time work when you come into New Zealand is really helpful in getting you out and interacting with people and building contacts. I felt, initially that I needed to be at home to help the kids settle etc. Of course, they settled far more quickly than Mike or I and the act of going to a job and mixing and meeting with people really did stop me from feeling so lonely and a little bit isolated. I would recommend it to any ladies out there - it really does help!

Having said that, when I worked in the nursery it was very clear that it was not right. I had a sensation of standing in a bubble with no sound, but the vision of everyone rushing past me as if I did not exist. It was very weird and a little disturbing, but graphically told me that this was not the right place for me, although I had very much looked forward to looking after young children!

The photo that made centre page spread of the Sunday Time Magazine – story was about people "flooding" out of the UK (predicted to be over 600,000 by 2011) October 2004

More magazine work –East End Beach, New Zealand

The family pictured for the Taranaki Daily News after being "crowned" Champion Migrants of The World by Outbound Publishing, UK – November 2005

Mike's personalised number plate – Mutley being his nickname – plate cost $500 – car stolen in Auckland and the only thing recovered were the number plates!

Alex's personalised plate – her Greek name! Plates can be
up to six characters and anything is possible as long as it
has not already been taken!

This is the new NZ family addition with Jake –
blackmailed in the UK by the kids Billy Spot "arrived" in
May 2006 – he is now somewhat bigger!

First attempt at our Christmas 2007 family photo-card –
note no shoes!

Dam dropping with Taranaki Outdoor Adventures, July 2005. A present to Mike's UK based sister on her wedding anniversary!

Part of the clan at Queenstown, July 2008 with Lake
Wakatipa behind

The Cole Family and Mayor of New Plymouth, Peter Tennent,
at the citizenship ceremony where we officially became Kiwis
– August 2007

Gabs, Mike, Jake, Guest of Honour Papoo and Alex ready to jet boat to the Huka Falls, Taupo – November 2008. Papoo is Greek for grandfather!

Jake with Piri Weepu All Black scrum-half. The ABs visited Jake's school prior to playing Samoa in New Plymouth! September 2008

The All Blacks in New Plymouth – live.

Performing the Haka

The boys after a job well done!

The game over and victory secured.

Ritchie McCaw injured but still a strong
part of the team.

PART 5

CREATING BRITSNZ

BritsNZ – from where did it spring? The simple answer is necessity!

After ten months of trying to build a client base, with no positivity from the people I initially came to work for and with not much additional income generated, hard decisions had to be made about how we would earn money and secure our life in New Zealand.

Both Alex and I had "put fingers in pies", doing anything and everything to earn some money and whilst we had a great time (both at the time and, of course, on reflection) and did things we'd never have done normally, we needed to find something that we could do longer term.

Whilst I had been very keen to "change my life" by moving to New Zealand and in my mind had seen that as not having to work in financial services, it was, of course, what I knew best and so, to a degree, was a sensible option to investigate.

By this time, we had also been involved in the video diary, which made us realise we could open doors and that we had a story to tell. The response to our new website was testimony to that, even though it was relatively amateurish in design compared to what we have now. It was bringing people to us but, as is the way of things, we did not actually see what was in front of us initially.

Having been through a "process" to create the name BritsNZ and the logo – all done by Alex and me - we then decided that we should focus on financial matters under a company umbrella of BritsNZ Ltd, using the logo we had created.

The help we got from a guy called Tran Lawrence, who ran a company called Taranaki Outdoor Adventures (Alex and I had both worked for him – me cooking which was great fun – and our daughters were friends) was amazing and welcome. He helped create that first website and, importantly, took two computer morons into the new century and allowed us to work on it ourselves, thus saving us a huge amount of dosh! He also advised us to trademark our name and logo which was also invaluable.

So, we had a company name and logo and, with the help of our friend and lawyer, Garry Anderson, had, within less than two hours total, a Limited Company set up with everything legally in place that allowed us to trade!

The next task was to bring the New Zealand insurance companies on board. Here I had huge help from a member of the Sovereign business development team, who helped me open an Agency with Sovereign and then introduced me to three Directors running a company called Paragon Insurance.

You could not hope to meet three more chilled characters to work alongside as we created our business. They were incredibly open to my ideas and plans on how I wanted to operate and went out of their way to help. This effectively gave me a physical base to work from and effected additional introductions to other providers with whom I was able to open Agencies.

Between us we managed to hammer out an agreement for BritsNZ's and Paragon's business relationship – again this took hours in reality and not days and so in no time we were up and operating, which was all well and good but of course we wanted clients.

I think one of the reasons we were so successful was that none of what we did initially was "scripted", which meant we were always open-minded and went with the flow and our timing always seemed to be about right. For example, within a couple of months of getting the website running and the business formalised, we received a formal invitation (with sponsorship in place) to come back to the UK and speak at emigration seminars – suddenly a client base was opening for us!

Initially, we started by working our local contacts and, relatively early on, had business to do.

Another interesting issue is the way that lessons come to you.

One of those very early clients had me do the bulk of the work and then screwed me on the price I was charging, even though it had been made abundantly clear and accepted at the outset. They quite rightly saw that I was over a barrel and decide to squeeze and, at that time being "desperate" for income, I caved and discounted my fee. The point is that the incident made us talk about what we would do next time. As the whole episode had pissed me off greatly, we determined that there would not be a next time; I would rather walk than have someone treat me like that – and do you know, as it's my business I can do just that! However, in those early days we were constantly worrying about whether we would ever have another client, but we were always alert to lessons to be learnt!

Whilst all this was happening, the video diary we had worked on was finished and a copy arrived on our doorstep. Much to our amazement, it had turned into a competition and all the participants were being "judged" by a panel of experts looking for the family they thought was the best prepared and the most likely to succeed and the buying public were being invited to vote on-line! It was very pleasing to find that all the judges were giving us a big thumbs-up – this would again be a big boost to our business but perhaps more importantly the general buying public were also voting for us!

In addition we were getting more and more email traffic from our website, helped by the video and newspaper articles in the Destination New Zealand newspaper and whilst there were a number of queries relating to financial issues, most were about emigrating in general!

We were always very focused on getting back to people as quickly as we could and to provide as much input as we could, covering all the topics we could and referring people on whenever we needed to. We soon learnt another lesson and it resonated with something I had once read, supposedly attributed to Richard Branson I believe, which was that the "perfect" business was one where you earned money whilst sleeping, so we gradually built a series of contacts and partners in the UK so we could endeavour to do just that. However, we have always been very, very focused on making sure that those we partner with have the same work and customer service ethics as ourselves and that we dealt with the people at the top so that we could make things happen for our clients if the need arose!

We had also at the outset agreed that we would always paint a true picture of life in New Zealand – we have never been into the rose-tinted glasses approach, as it is hard enough to emigrate without arriving to find that what you expected is not what you're getting. This truth-telling aspect was something we did even when it was obvious that we were saying things that people did not want to hear – we wanted to know that we had at least done our very best to paint the right picture for people!

So, we came to a crunch (another "lesson" time!) and this will probably sound weird, bearing in mind that we were running a business and being commercial – or supposedly so! We absolutely struggled with the idea of charging for our services – the financial side was easier, as we could both fully see the service and benefit to people and, if you like, it was a common/familiar aspect of life. Migration services were another ball game.

Fortunately, we had some awesome friends in the UK, Karen and Peter Goadby, who understood the situation and had a knack of painting a picture that both Alex and I could see and understand, but there was still a weird feeling about charging for the migration input. We understood the logic but until we had a few people start paying us for our time we still felt odd about it. In fact, and to be honest, it probably took us over two years to really get a fee structure that we were comfortable with, that clients were happy with and that we knew, based on the high levels of service, gave awesome value for money!

 ## BRITSNZ AT THE EMIGRATE SHOWS

So far, we were giving advice on people's financial and physical migration. We attended two shows where we were being "sponsored" back to talk and then, realising where our core business was coming from, we opted to take stands in our own right as BritsNZ.

The first time we did this we arranged for Alex to have a couple of weeks in the UK before the show. I arrived the eve of the show and we put Alex back on the plane on the Sunday immediately afterwards – thankfully, we found people mad enough to agree to have our three kids for six nights, thereby enabling all this to happen.

After that, I came up to the UK by myself to man the stand and talk to people and also speak at a series of seminars: these were invaluable to us as they put me in front of people focused on coming down to New Zealand to start a new life. Interestingly, I have always seen these seminars as information-giving, rather than as a vehicle for selling my company and I have had more than one person tell me to be more commercial and to really push what we do. I still quite strongly feel that my role is to tell people what they can expect; sure, I tell them in broad details what BritsNZ does, but I know from experience that because I tend to be one of very few companies up from New Zealand and, most importantly, am a migrant myself, people will find us out and talk to me. In fact, I know enough other exhibitors at the show that I now have them saying, "if you are looking at New Zealand, go and see Mike Cole. He's done it himself and can help you" – best advertising a company can get!

We are always looking for, and at, opportunities with regard to advertising and shows and whilst our mainstay show is the Emigrate Shows, (go and see their website at www.emigrate2.co.uk) as it links to the Emigrate New Zealand newspaper in which we advertise and for which we write articles, we have looked at other options too.

The Emigrate Shows are broken into two seasons: spring (meaning February and March); and autumn (meaning September and October) and are held in Edinburgh, at Sandown Racecourse, and in Belfast (spring) and then Liverpool and Coventry (autumn).

I recognised early on that in order to run both the stand and speak at the seminars, I needed help, since leaving the stand unattended meant we were missing people and, therefore, opportunities.

We started off looking for temps, but the issue here was that they knew nothing of New Zealand – I could quite quickly explain what we do as a company and what I needed the temp to do (get people to complete an information form), but what people wanted was to speak about New Zealand. We have been very fortunate that at some of the shows we have been offered help by clients who have experienced our service and, most importantly, who have been to New Zealand and so can be insightful in their comments about New Zealand and what people should/could expect. Our immense thanks must go to Debbie and Eckart Von Beck, and Niall and Pippa Ward, Jack Readhead who were all totally magnificent, your help was massive: respect!

We did also strike gold this year by finding a temp who was actually a Kiwi, an Auckland girl (but you can't hold that against her!) on her OE (overseas experience) trip and who is a bright as a button. Katie O'Hara, at the risk of swelling your head, your enthusiasm and quickness to learn what we are all about and then to get that across in your own inimitable style was frankly awesome!

We have also refined what our stand looks like at the shows and, with the help of Ambrose from The Marketing Company here in New Plymouth, we now have a very professional looking stand, great, high quality literature and photos – we are definitely "the business"!

One thing about the shows that never fails to amaze me is the reaction from other exhibitors: are we in competition? Yes, we are, but there are more than enough people wanting to migrate to New Zealand to keep all of us extremely busy and I have always felt it is better to work harmoniously and collaboratively to the benefit of the migrant – emigrating is hard enough without there being added layers of stress caused by exhibitors battling with each other!

Having said that, I have been fortunate to often have crowds around my stand and, given the company name, BritsNZ, it's pretty obvious that people waiting to speak with me/my helpers are heading to New Zealand, and yet other exhibitors want to know what we do and where we are taking people – er...hallo!

I remember one year in particular where we had a mix up with our stand size – we got a smaller one than had been ordered, which meant that people were queuing out in the passageways and onto other stands. One removals company (yes, a removals company) got the dog because people waiting to see me were on and around their stand. In fact, they asked us to do something about moving people off and away from their stand. Do you know, not ONCE did the people on that stand start talking to the people waiting to see me about their removal needs to New Zealand – talk about ignoring the gift horse!

These shows are crucial to our business and are amazing events. The people we get to meet across a huge swathe of society and job skills is fantastic and it is liberating to see people with the passion that we felt about leaving and making life changing decisions – often it is quite humbling to know that we can actually help make dreams a reality!

I totally enjoy the shows, meeting new people, speaking at seminars to hopefully convey the passion we feel for New Zealand and helping people realise that, with determination, almost everyone can turn a dream into something tangible.

Away from the show, we know only too well from our move that you often make your own "luck" and that often what you need comes to you if you ask. We have been extremely fortunate in the people we have invited into our business as consultants.

In the first instance we were recommended to speak to a chap called Saul Ireland who looks at systems – not necessarily computer systems, but how to get a potential client from nothing to business. He has a unique way of working which can cause heart palpitations: effectively, he listens to what you do as a business and then looks at you as an individual and your role in the company. Here he was a godsend, as he allowed Alex and me to more clearly define what each of us needed to do. He then proceeds to tip everything on, in, around or vaguely near your desk onto the floor and asks you to justify why you have it and how important it is to you. At first it is incredibly threatening but, by the end, it's totally liberating, as the mess has gone, you know what you have and why and suddenly your ability to work is more harmonious and "easy"!

During this process Saul (in his own words) was fortunate (he actually said privileged but that sounds terribly pretentious!) to hear me speaking for over an hour to someone in the UK. That gave him a total insight into what we do and what we were trying to achieve and he "built" systems to make things more orderly and to work for us.

Saul then introduced us to Ambrose Blowfield, who is a marketing man, who came and looked at what we did and tried to identify (successfully) what we were looking to achieve and how to get the best return for our marketing spend.

Initially, he was a bit like a whirling dervish but we soon cut the pace back a bit. Where was our business plan? Er...yeah, right! Who were our target market? Mmmmm! What were our targets for numbers of leads from shows? Ho ho ho!

I feared that perhaps initially Ambrose would think us too laid back, but after delving deeper into us and the company he recognised that, in fact, part of our success was in not being limited to, or by, a business plan and that made us much more adaptable to change and taking opportunities as they arose! He also recognised that we had some strong views but were always prepared to listen and be flexible – after all why would we not be, given that we were paying for his expertise!

Crucially, Ambrose moved us into a completely new focus with our marketing material – we became far more professional in the way we did all things marketing and I think that anyone seeing our stand at the shows and looking at our literature would agree that we have a great visual impact – our colours are bold and our literature is of high quality.

Without doubt, our focus has changed and we have become sharper at what we do and in the way we do it, but ultimately we are here to help, and to help at a time when people are making life changing moves, and we NEVER forget that: to be honest, we are still able to easily put ourselves back (emotionally) into the position we were in when moving and often when speaking with people those emotions well up and it is like we are doing it all again.

We love what we do with an absolute passion and I think it is fair to say that it has been four years of continuously hard but extremely rewarding work. Yes, we have been successful, but in our work that is not measured purely by the bank balance but by seeing the joy people get when they get their visas and then seeing them grasping their new lives in New Zealand. We are both fortunate and extremely privileged to see and be part of these transformations!

It is only now, after four years, that we are actually claiming our lives back from our business a bit. In the first two years I did not take a day off (no, I am not intending to brag, but rather show the dedication and passion we gave to our business) and not very many since then. (The curse of computers, the Internet and phones is that you are never away: it's always with you!) Thankfully, by the very nature of skiing in New Zealand (i.e. you don't live on the slopes as in Europe and the Americas) meant we had to drive to get to the ski fields, so that very much limited our "working" time whilst in Queenstown recently to about an hour a day and that was just a fantastic break for us.

So what does the future hold? Who knows for sure? We will remain dedicated and focused on helping people realise their dreams and will continue to look at opportunities, both within the emigration market and elsewhere. When we left the UK, Alex and I made a promise to each other that we would always look carefully at every opportunity that came our way and, with perhaps one or two exceptions, we have done just that and, as a result, have created our successes.

We are always available to people looking to make a dream come true, no matter to which country, and you can access us through our website at www.britsnz.co.nz or via e-mail on info@britsnz.co.nz

A poster of the family at Sandown Racecourse Emigrate March 2005 – this was a huge boost to our business but it was weird to look at and even more weird to see people nudge each other and look twice at us!

BritsNZ stand at an Emigrate Show event.

NEWSPAPER ARTICLES

14/6/2006

Things Come in Threes!

So there you are, believing everything is going along well. Your new business is doing very well, you have had a successful trip back to the UK for the March emigrate shows, you've just had four days with old friends in Singapore and now it's back to the family and some late summer sunshine!

That's when the guy above decides to have a laugh and everything crumbles around you!

So here's the list of misfortunes that threatened my sanity for a while but never, not even for one second, dimmed my excitement and passion for New Zealand, particularly once home to great surf beaches and a totally awesome mountain!

- I arrived back from the airport to find a dent in the driver's door of my car which had been parked on the drive whilst I was away. The lovely and slim Mrs Cole denied doing it and the kids swore blind it wasn't them. Ho hum!

- Whilst juggling helping with homework, speaking on the phone and cooking supper, I managed to badly burn my arm with very hot oil – hard to keep your arm under the cold water when you are hopping from foot to foot and not swearing too badly in front of the kids!

- Three days into being home, still jet-lagged and now burnt, the computer starts to make very peculiar noises (thought it might be one of the kids with wind at first!) and stops working. On inspection, a crashed hard drive is diagnosed (first of its kind in New Zealand for that laptop – the one occasion when being first is really not all its cracked up to be!) and sad to say I'd not quite gotten around to doing a back-up, so I lost three weeks of data, work, leads and one hundred and sixty-six e-mails – because, of course, I'd had problems sending e-mail from the UK (I'm seeing Vodafone in person next week to wring some necks!) and so had a back log. No quibble about the hard drive as it was still in warranty but we sent the old one to a forensics company in Auckland.

- The forensics company in Auckland call four days later to say "Oops. You need some new drivers mate" (you what??) and kindly put me in touch with a chap who tells me that he can get them from the good old USA at $700 – this of course turned out to be $800 (mugged again) but I needed that data. Suffice to say the forensics guys fitted new drivers and turned it all on and BANG......$880 up in smoke and all my data lost and some three weeks gone by. I had that sort of Titanic sinking feeling!

- As part of my fiftieth birthday celebrations (I know I don't look it and I have raised the issue of the year of birth with my parents) my lovely wife arranged a superb trip to Oz for us a family – the first break we'd have taken in nearly two years and having celebrated for two days with late nights partying and time spent up the mountain (an aside here – we went up Mt Taranaki on Good Friday (my birthday) with cloudless blue skies and fresh snow on the top and we could see clear across the North Island to Mt Ruapehu, also snow covered – it was simply stunning and we stood in awe of the beauty around us and again had it reinforced just what a truly amazing country we have the privilege of living in) I managed to set the alarm for an early get up and to check the time on the clock and then promptly forgot to flick the switch to actually turn the alarm on!

- Our flight was at 7 a.m. from New Plymouth to Auckland connecting for Brisbane and I woke at 6.36! Well, the Keystone Cops had nothing on us...Kids were woken and told to simply dress and get in the car as we were late, Joe (our eldest) jumped out of bed and fell flat on the floor as he'd not registered a dead leg and had to crawl to the loo!

- As Alex flew through the house with a suitcase behind her, she shouted to me, "Mike! Bring the other case, blah, blah, blah". Doing as I was told, I grabbed the case and realised "blah, blah, blah" translated into "zip it up first". So, of course, everything crashed out and was simply scooped back in and thrown in the car, along with the phone book.

- We then sped across the city with Alex on the phone trying to get the airport to hold the flight – we are a small enough place that these things are possible - but the number just would not connect. In desperation, we called a car hire booth who insisted on giving us the number we already knew, but finally persuaded them to get the Air NZ girl onto the phone who told us we were literally one minute too late, as the door was closed and the plane was taxiing and - sure enough - as we turned onto the airport road the plane soared into the crystal clear sky and that vortex sure looked like two fingers!

- Got to terminal to find no other flights would be through in time to connect in Auckland so it was an hour on the phone to Air NZ re-booking and as Alex had booked using air miles we were literally re-booking the flights at a cost and what a cost – an additional $2,500 for the five of us!

- Guess who was not popular even though it was my birthday and I could ruin it if I wanted… Thankfully, whilst having a MacyDs breakfast Alex started laughing as she suddenly envisaged us as the "Home Alone" family as we could so easily have left a child behind!

- Finally, five weeks ago I was working up in Auckland for a week, staying with a friend in Howich. I got up on Friday morning to drive back home and where was my car?? I walked up the drive and out onto the street but no car. So, thinks me, it must be on the drive. No, you muppet, you just walked up the drive and it wasn't there. Yep some kind Aucklander decided that what was mine was actually theirs and I thought that rule only applied in the sanctity of marriage!

- So, much hassle and many phone calls later, I was on my way to the airport having done a trade with the insurers so I could fly home instead of driving. Mind you, the flight was only booked after Alex spoke with our psychic friend, as by then paranoia had set in very firmly.

- My son found it amazing that I was so calm about having the car stolen but by then the sequence was so entrenched that my thought was, "Yep, that will be about right!"

- Of course, there have now been battles with insurers and although they were very happy to insure it on a professional valuation nine months ago at $19,000, I only managed after some 'harsh' words to get them to $15,000 which will not buy a similar replacement car and of course there is all the hassle of replacing everything that was in it – and how hard is that? How many of you could sit down now and write a list of what's in your car with any great accuracy? Anyways up, I have a new car on order and will be going down to Wellington on the 23rd to pick it up. It's a... now, that would be telling!

Through all this there have been some very black moments and, in hindsight, very funny moments but it has cost us quite some money and the morals from this are:

- Back up your computer regularly and definitely before you leave the UK.
- Don't cook and do multiple other things – leave that to the ladies!
- If you are going to set the alarm turn the blessed thing on!

- Check that your insurance will actually do what you believe it will do. Ours did not quite do that and it was fortunate I could exert some pressure on the insurer.
- Put a GPS tracking system in your car...! Only partially joking!
- Keep smiling, because you do come out of these periods and have some great material for an article or after dinner speech!

9th April 2005

Emigrating with Kids

G'day everyone.

This is Mike and Alex Cole here from the Emigrate Challenge DVD. We have just been fortunate enough to go to the Emigrate 2005 Show at Sandown Racecourse to talk to people about our experiences and answer any questions they had about the whole emigration process.

There was one question which stood out for us from the show: how do we tell our kids of our plans and dreams, and also how do we tell our family and friends?

To be honest, this issue threw us somewhat as we had never, at any time, kept our hopes and dreams and plans 'secret' from our kids or other immediate family. Of course, as we progressed we had a number of different reactions and at times suffered some discreet and some not so discreet emotional blackmail.

This is part of the process and our advice is to face it early on but always keep in mind why YOU want to go and simply "ride the storm". Remember, if family and friends cannot accept your reasoning that is their problem, not yours!

This very much goes for your children. We involved ours all the way through by openly talking about what we were doing, why we were doing it and getting them involved in making decisions and looking at things on the net concerning New Zealand.

We have three kids: Joe, twelve, Jake, eight and Gabs, three (ages shown at the time we left the UK). To be honest, the younger they are the easier it appears to be for them. Certainly Gabs has made the transition the best, as she had not built the really close bonds of friendships that the other two had. Jake seemed to make the move relatively easily on the outside but we know he holds things close so have been careful to make sure he is doing okay with his new environment. Our eldest was the dark horse – the most positive about leaving the UK but instantly on arrival in New Zealand the most unsettled. Typical teenager perhaps...?

As for us adults, the reality of saying goodbye to all our friends was particularly difficult. We made sure (correctly/incorrectly…who knows?) that both the boys had parties of sorts where they could go and be 'free' to have a great time with friends but the actual leaving was very difficult, perhaps more so for Joe who was receiving multiple texts from his mates right to the point of getting on the plane!

So, having left the UK, we look back and say:

- Involve the kids from the outset
- Give them tasks to do on the net about their soon-to-be new home
- Allow them to express their views, but remember why you wanted to make this move and keep focused…kids are very good at playing you off against each other or family members!
- Try and make the goodbyes fun but not dragged out
- We very strongly recommend having the night before at Heathrow so you can get over the emotional stress of saying goodbye and not suffer the travel stress of just getting to Heathrow on time. To our mind, this is money extremely well spent. We also know that NOT having family at the airport makes the real leaving just that little bit easier, particularly when you have a long journey ahead of you.

Once in your new country there are decisions to be made for/by the kids so again involve them.

The initial key decision is schooling. We had done the research in the UK about the schools in New Plymouth, where we were to settle, and knew there was a choice between single-sex schooling and co-ed schooling. Joe, when asked, had opted for the co-ed high school so as to replicate the environment we had moved him from. Once in New Plymouth we looked at both schools and sought the comments of local people as to their merits. Local input is very helpful, so seek it out!

In the end, we were happy to allow him to go to the co-ed school. With that sorted we found a primary school literally just down the road from the high school and visited it with our middle child. We were shown around and loved the feel of the place and - crucially - so did our son, so, effectively, both boys chose where they went to school...and why not, as they are the ones going, not us!

One final point about schools is that we found the New Zealand schools were slightly behind where the boys had been in the UK. We actually saw this as a positive in the sense that it took some pressure off them in the classroom and perhaps allowed them to settle more easily initially.

For Gabs, the issues were in finding a Kindy (nursery) and in this we simply asked our motel owner who had kids of a similar age and went with her advice. This turned out to be a shrewd move as Gabs is very, very happy. Again the calculated 'gamble' of using local knowledge paid off.

The other thing about your kids is to look at what they do in the UK and see if they can do the same in your new country. BUT doing the same thing may not be as easy as it seems, so be prepared for upset children when you least expect it. An example: Joe is a very good footballer (well, with a name like Joe Cole he would be, wouldn't he?!) and so we decided that we'd try and get him into the best local team, but he wouldn't have it at all and got very, very upset. It was at this point we realised that for eight years he'd always played with the same kids all the way through the grades and to go somewhere new, where he knew no one, was a totally daunting thing for him and something we had not twigged until then. This was resolved by sitting down with him and sorting out what he wanted. Eventually he had an awesome season playing for the school!

One other thing to be aware of with your kids is to be careful what you promise, because they NEVER forget! Interestingly, we have found we are not alone in making 'promises' about what they can do and have once in their new home. Let's be honest, a bit of blackmail is the main incentive option for loads of us parents! If you promise a dog, they'll remember. If you promise horse-riding lessons, they'll remember. If you promise they will do homework every night they'll definitely NOT remember!

We had been away from the UK for eighteen months and when we agreed to return for the Emigrate Show, we opted to bring the kids back. In hindsight this was not a great idea. We felt, as adults, we were coming back too soon and this has proved doubly true for the kids. Being back in the UK has been extremely unsettling and all have been in tears about having to say goodbye to friends again. We have been here for five weeks, which is too long, particularly with all the travelling we have done to see friends and have business meetings. The kids have borne up well but we know in our hearts that we have come back too soon and stayed too long. Thankfully we have the 'bribe' of a holiday in LA and Disney on the way back but it's going to be horribly difficult to say goodbye again.

Is there a magic time to make that first trip back? We have no idea, but we believe that eighteen months away was NOT long enough. The boys were really settling well (it had been a difficult twelve months for Joe and he seemed to come through it and get well settled, so the timing for him was really poor) having had a totally awesome summer and they were seeing their own home starting to be built.

It will not be the same for everyone, but we would imagine that perhaps it would have been better after two-and-a-half or three years. This is difficult to judge, so just be warned that coming back too soon can cause problems for you and the kids. We will have to let you know how they settle back into New Zealand in a future edition!

For the full story of our emigration either go to the Destination website and get the Emigrate Challenge DVD and/or go onto our website at www.britsnz.co.nz where you will find the story and useful hints and ideas to help you through the whole process. We are always available by e-mail on britsnz@inspire.net.nz, so by all means do touch base with us.

Good luck with your emigration journey and - who knows - perhaps we'll meet in New Zealand one day!

Mike & Alex Cole

April 2008

Communicating from/to New Zealand

What!! Where am I?? What is that noise?? It's the mobile phone. Stagger out of bed, hit the wall (thank you, now I know roughly where I am), fall through the door, as I get there sooner than I thought. Pick myself up, follow the sound until I can crank an eye open to see the flashing light...Oh my gawd, it's 1.30 a.m. I am jetlagged beyond belief and am assuming I am actually in my own home. Look at the screen - it's the UK. Could this be something to do with Alex's parents? I press answer and croak "Hallo." A very strange voice goes, "Oh gosh. I have just realised the time. Have I woken you?" (Er, yep!). "We just needed to speak with you about moving to New Zealand. Shall I call you back in your morning?" (Er, yep!)

The above actually did happen to me just after I arrived back from the UK and highlights one of the key things that people need to get their heads around – the time difference! Sure you can call easily and cheaply from/to New Zealand, but getting the time right is the difficulty, especially at this time of year and in October, when the clocks are changing. At this time (2 April), New Zealand is twelve hours ahead of the UK, with you guys having just changed your clocks to summer time. However, this weekend New Zealand puts the clocks back to go onto winter time, so, from Sunday, we will be eleven hours ahead. And this all then works in reverse in October when we end up being +13 hours!

So, just how can you stay in touch with family and friends, for pleasure or for business purposes?

Needless to say, one of the easiest ways is via the Internet, and with broadband available in most areas the link can be quick and faultless. With broadband you can then set up webcams so it's not just a question of speaking but also of seeing. For the folks back home, particularly grandparents, this is invaluable, as it brings you so much closer.

A hint for soon-to-be migrants would be to make sure your parents have access to the Internet and perhaps get them a webcam as a "leaving" present. Just make sure you buy it well before you go so that they (and you) can practice!

Now, with webcams you can use either MSN Messenger or SKYPE...we tend to prefer SKYPE as it not only allows you to talk computer-to-computer, but by buying "credit" you can very cheaply call landlines and mobiles both within New Zealand and, of course, to the UK. Currently, a call to the UK will cost about 0.017 cents a minute!

Of course, there is the trusty old telephone and here in New Zealand you can get a series of different options to call the UK at sensible rates. We use Slingshot, who not only provide our broadband Internet connection but also cheap rate toll calls, so we can call the UK for two hours for $4!

There are occasions when the mobile networks also offer deals. Vodafone has recently done a deal whereby a half hour call from your mobile to the UK was $2!

Of course, there is always that dreaded call at an obviously "wrong" time when someone from the UK is calling with bad news, but I'm afraid that is all part and parcel of emigrating – it's not a question of "if" but rather "when" and at least there are now insurances you can take that will get you back to the UK for a small annual premium (about £175) so you and your family in the UK can buy this added peace of mind.

I must admit that the friends I stay with in the UK were somewhat disappointed this time as it must be the first time that my good wife, Alex, and I have not had a blazing row down the phone with each being half a world away! On the other hand I can still tell the kids off, pull my eldest back into line by speaking with them or texting them...how does that work?!

Once you have family on the other side of the world you obviously need to be somewhat more organised with birthdays and Christmas so that you catch the post just right. Letters by air mail will take some seven days, whilst snail mail across the surface of the world will take around six plus weeks. Usually, at Christmas, there is plenty of notice given as to when the last posting date is so you can plan quite carefully!

As with most things, staying in touch is a state of mind but for those coming to New Zealand I would suggest that it is a two-way street: simply because you left this does not mean that the sole emphasis remains with you, so do your "deals" on who calls who when etc before you leave, as it can get very wearing to always be driving the staying-in-contact aspects of your life!

June 2008

Emigrate NZ

The big question at the moment is: does an economic downturn affect emigration?

One would imagine that such a downturn simply highlights more of the reasons people have for leaving and perhaps gives the extra "push" to make people take the first steps. But then, does it hinder you actually leaving?

Of course, one area that will be affected is the ability for people to sell their houses and realise the capital they have accumulated and which will aid their emigration.

In general terms here at BritsNZ, we recommend that people do look to sell their house prior to taking the emigration road to New Zealand (or anywhere else for that matter!) – emigrating is as much a mental process as a physical process and migrants need to have their heads and hearts looking at the move as permanent, and to do that people need to "cut ties" and "burn bridges". There will be tough times on reaching your new country - after all you will be a foreigner in a foreign land and things do not always go as smoothly as we would all like - and it is at those times that not having an easily accessible "bolt hole" can make all the difference!

At this time, of course, the housing market in the UK is being portrayed as dire, but in our experience more people to this point in the year have sold their homes than at the same point last year. To be fair, we had noticed issues within the housing market for probably the last twelve months and you have to wonder whether the lack of sales in migrant's homes was reflective of asking too much for their houses (and we fully acknowledge that you absolutely need to get the most you can from this, your biggest asset, but there is always a time when you have to assess whether it is more important to be in New Zealand or get an extra amount for your house, particularly if that causes delays in coming to New Zealand). We have certainly seen people hanging out for a bit more money who have then "upset" their prospective new Kiwi employer by delaying so long that the job offer gets removed, with all the consequences that has for visas etc!

The issue of whether to sell at all costs is a tough one and ultimately only you can make that call and given the current market in the UK and the strength of the NZ$ everything appears to working against you just now. This would indicate that perhaps renting is the way to go. In my opinion if you really are not happy to sell now, then rent, but do not get drawn into a long term rental agreement: we know of some recent migrants who have got themselves locked into a three-year deal – this is just too long and creates issues here in New Zealand which could have perhaps been avoided by a shorter term agreement. The issues here in New Zealand are either that you are locking into long-term renting or you are having to take a bigger mortgage, and with floating mortgage rates in New Zealand being around 10.7% that is both expensive and painful!

If renting is the option you choose, then look at putting in place rental agreements for a series of six months. In all likelihood, you will retain the same tenant and it is important that you retain the flexibility of being able to put your house on the market when you want to do so. Also, if you do rent, use a reputable agent – they should mention a thing called the Landlord Abroad scheme and you can do some research by following these links: www.hmrc.gov.uk.cnr/nrl1.pdf
and http://www.hmrc.gov.uk/cnr/nr_landlords.htm

With the exchange rate as it stands just now, even if you do sell your house you may need to exercise patience – at this time we do not see interest rates falling in New Zealand until September at the earliest and more likely the end of the year. New Zealand has the highest interest rates (apart from South Africa) in the "developed" world and it will take either a significant event (such as the sub-prime issues last year) or a resurgence in strength in the USA and a drop in interest rates here to weaken the NZ$. You will obviously need to change some money as you need to set up your lives again in New Zealand, but you simply need to identify a strategy for your currency exchange(s) and stick with it!

On the up-beat side of things (from your view point in the UK), we are seeing property prices coming off the boil here in New Zealand and in some areas price deflation, principally in the major cities just now (the general view is that Auckland will suffer most), so it is very much now a buyer's market and if we can get the NZ$ weakening next year there may be some "bargains" for new migrants who have cash in hand!

The current housing decline and economic slowdown is a worldwide issue – how much of it is a reality and how much media hype we'll not truly know until hindsight clicks in, but it is interesting that the US (very much more badly hit by sub-prime than anywhere else) appears to be at least stable now, whereas Britain still seems to be suffering. Whether that is a character trait, an overactive doom-laden media, or simply a reflection of the current political malaise I cannot be sure, but one thing is for sure; unless and until Britain gets its self-belief back and gets some positive news flowing through the media it could be a struggle for migrants to sell their properties, particularly if they are looking to squeeze every last penny from their bricks and mortar!

Queenstown or Bust! – July 2008

Planning is everything and we'd done everything necessary.

Brief – family ski trip to Queenstown.

First, accommodation. Easy! My NZ professional body (The Professional Advisers Association) have various holiday homes, including one in Queenstown and Alex – who arranges things - got online and booked nine nights. A year out and we had the accommodation organised.

Flights. More luck - direct flights to Christchurch (CHCH) had just started – booked in, no problem.

Eight months out, flights and accommodation organised – impressive.

The rot started four months out.

I realised that the plan involved eight hours' driving, meaning arrival in Queenstown at 11 p.m. Not a great idea, driving through mountains in the dark – the roads are awful.

Solution – one-way flight (driving back; we'd have a couple of days to play with) from CHCH to Queenstown.

All organised – flights from New Plymouth to CHCH, on to Queenstown, car rental there to take back to CHCH, then fly directly to New Plymouth.

More "rot" – a call a week before from Air New Zealand Link, saying the direct flight had been cancelled and we now had to go via Wellington. Okay, would only add forty minutes to the trip.

Then finding out that the Friday we flew, industrial action was being taken by pilots, but were assured that no flights would be cancelled...

Bags packed, kids in tow (happily out of school a day early: planning - travel before end of term!) Off we go. The sun shines - perfect day for travelling. Mount Taranaki looks stunning, sun glinting off snow. No problems flying into Wellington. No problems with the connecting flight – so far everything on time. Just quiet mutterings from the airport and TV weather reports about a storm blowing in from the pole – nothing like a southerly to mess things up.

Arriving in sunshine in CHCH and boarding the next flight on time. Sitting there...sitting there...hearts sinking...sitting there! Finally the Captain announces that they are waiting for two passengers (thirty minutes for a missing passenger? Where else in the world??)

"By the way, the storm from the south is making things a bit tight getting into Queenstown."

Ten minutes later, he says the missing passengers' bags must be removed and that (again as an aside) the weather window is shrinking quickly.

Five minutes more and - BANG – he states the window has closed and the flight is cancelled.

Amongst the ensuing chaos we agree that Alex should run for it and get us booked for the next day. I marshall the kids and hand luggage and follow behind. We finally get off and Alex is queuing and desperate for my phone to call the airline. Apparently, the most efficient way to re-book seats – call the airline, re-book for tomorrow, get to the counter and they simply re-print the ticket. Works perfectly!

The airline was offering a coach to get people to Queenstown: two things against that:

- Eight plus hours on a coach with three kids and arriving into Queenstown at midnight/1 a.m.

- No guarantee we would get through – the weather report was awful and if we got to the Lindis Pass (a four-hour drive) to find it closed, we could end up being on a coach for eight hours and back where we started.

Amongst the confusion, the boys went to rescue the bags and Gabs was put on carry-on luggage guard – she sat in the middle of the airport surrounded by our stuff and people trying to sort out their messed up plans, appearing oblivious to it all!

The boys returned minus one bag and, after extensive searching and questioning, the airline lost luggage office assured us it would appear, although they didn't know where it was: from New Plymouth to CHCH through Wellington and now missing – nice one!

It was chaotic and there was a total lack of urgency in looking for the bag. Clearly, they felt it had been unloaded and sent somewhere else in the airport – naturally, no one knew why our other two bags made it!

All this was overshadowed by the fact that Joe's girlfriend, Kelsi, who had decided relatively late to come with us, had flown earlier (our flights being full by the time she decided to come) and was in Queenstown alone. So we had a 15.5 year-old who had never flown before, or travelled by herself, alone in Queenstown: just a hint of desperation to get there. We called some friends, who luckily rescued the poor girl and looked after her. If anyone reading this knows Lee & Lara Fletcher they are RESCUE STARS!

We opted to stay in a hotel which the airline provided near the airport. Our international travel paid off here, as we knew what to say and do, whereas a number of others simply knew they could get a hotel room. Some thought they would need to pay – the airline had apparently been economical with the information. Therefore, the next morning the airline had a few people wanting their bills to be settled – oops!

The hotel was actually really good – even had a pool for the kids to play in – and our togs [Kiwi for swimmers] were not in the missing bag (all our wash gear but not our togs!) We had great family time reminiscing and laughing.

Next morning it's off to the airport for our 9 a.m. flight. The airport was crowded, as the holidays had started, plus all us delayed people trying to reach our destinations. I realised that frequent traveller cards have their privileges and we checked in through the "fast" route only to be told at the check-in that all flights south had been cancelled due to the weather and it was likely CHCH airport would also soon be closed.

Again, a window of opportunity to travel was offered:

- Dunedin or Invercargill, but we must make our own way to Queenstown and again the roads were said to be closed. Little point in going that route and why pay to get to your final destination by going out of your way!

- Return to New Plymouth. Start again. Eh? How does that work??

Again, we phoned The Rescuers in Queenstown and opted to stay in CHCH once we had booked another flight for tomorrow.

We rolled back into the hotel after another fruitless search for our bag, having been assured it would turn up soon and be delivered to the hotel. We convinced the hotel that we had indeed left and been forced to return. They slipped us back into the same rooms and the day lay ahead.

We went to investigate CHCH city centre and entered the "twilight zone"...

CHCH is the "capital" of the South Island and, whilst the school holidays had started AND it was very cold with the weather deteriorating, it was bizarre to be in a city centre at 11 a.m. on a Saturday and see no more than three dozen people – unimaginable in Birmingham or Manchester.

By 1.30 p.m. it was somewhat busier but by that time we'd had enough and returned to the hotel, then visited the Antarctic Exhibition near the airport.

Again, a bizarre experience.

We went for a ride in an Antarctic all-terrain vehicle. Gabs screamed and cried the whole way round – it was a rough ride – then demanded to do it all again. I'll NEVER understand girls!!

We went to see the penguins being fed, then went into the "freezer" to experience an Antarctic storm and look at the exhibits.

So, why bizarre? Because, apart from the actual storm episode it was more like the Antarctic outside, blowing a gale with snow pouring down and the whole area grinding to a halt – including the airport!

The burning question: would we get out next day? Oh, and where was our bag!

The next day, Sunday, (remember, we left home on Friday morning!) dawned wet and dull but we got to the airport to check in and ... Thunderbirds were GO!

Check-in went smoothly. I got everyone into the Koru Club (what, free Coke and food? How to make kids happy!) and we boarded on time, then sat for a while, hearts sinking but...no problems! We were off on the final forty-minute flight to Queenstown – yippee!!

As we fly out of CHCH the sun is shining, the mountains snow-covered - stunning - but we head south and west and the cloud builds. We expect no problems, however.

The pilot comes on as we near Queenstown: he will come in from the south on a long approach. We gently come down toward the airport for ages. Just when I thought, 'Okay, we must be nearly there', on goes the power, up come the wheels and we pull sharply up and away.

My tension builds, knowing this area is slap in the midst of mountains, but eventually the pilot comes on to say he wasn't comfortable with the weather and was now taking us to Invercargill – so close yet so far...And still one bag missing!

Landing in Invercargill, there were coaches to take us to Queenstown. We thought hiring a car would be a better choice, but whilst we plainly saw dozens of cars in the Hertz lot alone ALL the rental companies said they had none – yeah, right!

ANOTHER phone call to The Rescuers. They're at Queenstown airport and it appears that while our flight has not made it in, others have. Blood-boiling news and thoughts of conspiracy – was this the industrial action? Was it more convenient for the airline to have us anywhere other than in Queenstown?

Whatever, we were on a coach for a 2.5 hour trip. I played "I Spy" with Gabs for forty minutes and there really isn't a lot to "spy" on a coach. Still, we were together and the scenery was fantastic.

We pulled into Queenstown airport at 5 p.m., our 3.5 hour journey taking from 11 a.m. Friday until 5 p.m. Sunday, but we were there, Kelsi was safe and we were just missing one bag, which didn't turn up for another three days (so, lost for six days!!) – and no, I didn't smell but I did by then have an excess of toiletries!

Adding insult to injury, we had just arrived at the house when the whole place shook and there was a huge noise. Not an earthquake - the house was at the end of the runway and a jet was taking off over us and the lake. Glad someone was able to fly in/out of Queenstown that day...

We had some great down-time, some special family time and were, in fact, all pretty cooled out about the whole thing, plus we have a story we will never forget...And hey, the snow was awesome, the scenery stunning and a great time was had by all.

Oh, and we drove back through the centre of the South Island, via Wanaka to CHCH and flew home with no issues...and all our bags!

PART 6

THE THOUGHTS OF THOSE WE LEFT BEHIND!

We thought it would be a really good idea to let you have some feedback from those we left in the UK when we made the move – and it has been very interesting for us too!

We have been in contact with a good number of the people we knew and still know in the UK and asked then the following questions:

- What was your initial reaction when you heard our plans?
- How did you view the process of us working to get our Visas – did this impact on you in any way?
- What was your reaction when you heard that we had Visas and really were going?
- Were there any things you felt we could/should have done differently?
- Was there anything we did not handle very sensitively?
- How did you see our plans affecting the relationship we had with you?

- What was it like getting our letters in that first year – were they: 'welcome', 'informative', 'enlightening'?
- Did the letters ever give you cause for concern?
- Did you at any time think/believe we would not succeed and did you at any time believe we would come back to the UK?
- If you are aware that we have taken NZ citizenship what is your reaction to that news?

The idea is that the comments that follow may help you have an understanding of what those close to you may be thinking and feeling as you work hard to realise your dream and then head off to the other side of the ocean/world to make that new start!

Do remember that the dream is yours and you are actually only answerable to yourselves and your children and we are very much of the view that as long as you know why you are making this move and explain it as fully as you can when asked it is then no longer your "problem" if that friend/family member chooses not to embrace your plans and chooses instead to "not get it"!

Here are the comments we received (note that Dad is Greek and we are taking what he said exactly!):

What was your initial reaction when you heard our plans?

David: Thank God he is leaving the UK!

Angus: I first remember you and us discussing the thought of emigrating to NZ in the forest in Thetford at the Dower House. Drunk on fresh air, fortified by Mike's excellent cuisine and sharpened by the occasional sip of an excellent Rioja, I would suggest insane ways for us to pass the time, like moving around the world and looking for a lifestyle to get off the hamster wheel of the avaricious, conspicuous consumers - namely us in the UK.

I at no point expected you to do it!!!!!

Anyway, you and Mike went in to a furious Tasmanian devil of activity and then you were gone.

Now every time Mike returns I am green with envy at the relaxed, healthy, tanned relocation exec who visits us in the UK, with stories of lifestyle and plans to build a yet larger and more prestigious property all finished to an exceptional quality and spec. More big sighs of longing.

Mum:	Had to really think about it, but realised you were doing it for a better life for you and the children. Dad was very upset, but after all, he had left his family all those years ago hoping for a better life - whether he now thinks he has it or not, who knows?
Dad:	Very, very hard for me – split my heart in two!
John:	I was quite surprised at New Zealand. I had not heard of anyone emigrating there before. Given the size of the place and the population, I was unsure about how you would adapt to this environment.
Richard:	Having lived just up the road from you both, we obviously had early visibility of your plans and, whilst disappointed to lose lovely neighbours and friends, we were both delighted to learn that you intended to move to NZ to start the next chapter in your lives. As you know, Rosie has lived overseas in Dubai and Bermuda and so she, more than anyone, was sympathetic to the challenges and excitement a move like this brings and entails. We both knew that it would be a challenge, uprooting yourselves and

the children but you approached it in a methodical and very sensible way, committing to the project with sense and structure but also raw and unbridled enthusiasm. These were exciting times but careful planning and thought was given to the process, albeit I am sure that there are areas you would do things differently knowing what you know now. I am sure that clients of BRITSNZ are reaping the benefit of all that knowledge without perhaps realising the pain they are being spared.

Philip: Initial reaction was "this is a bit of a gamble Mike is taking with the ages of the children and the fact boys are at school", however there was the element of jealousy about you having the balls to go ahead and do it.

Lynne: We thought it was really exciting, though we were sorry to lose you.

DLD: Good on yer! More folks should make a move when they believe it would improve the quality of life for their family.

Bob & Yvonne: Our initial reaction - typical Alex and Mike always ones for a challenge and excitement.

Sister Les: Thought it was a good idea as I had already done the same thing twice!

Sister Jake: Disappointment that you thought the only way you could do better for your family was to haul them to the other side of the world. Looking back we could never understand when Equitable went down that you moved into exactly the same sector at Widows when you had always said how you didn't like the job. It was interesting that you chose a country that you hadn't visited until you had made the decision - but then we did wonder. (As a financial advisor you seemed to go against conventional wisdom in renting a house and stepping off the housing ladder when house prices were rising.)

How did you view the process of us working to get our visas – did this impact on you in any way?

David: No impact at all – only I had my fingers crossed for weeks on end!!

Mum: Not really

Dad: Not really, never bothered me!

John: Again, this was all so sudden, it seemed that as soon as I heard of you planning to go you were off to Manchester to get your visa. It all seemed too quick to be true, really.

Richard: Other than hearing about the process from you over beer and burgers at regular barbeques, we were largely unaffected by your efforts and activities but obviously interested and involved in discussions about the trials and tribulations. As much as we could, we listened, sympathised and criticised in harmony with you at the ease and pain of the various stages. It is obviously a difficult process and would have highs and lows along the way. Your resolute strength of character saw you through much of this process but it always helps to have friends around to share the experience with and to vent spleens, etc. Better to get all the joy and pain out with friends over a beer than to carry these emotions through into conversations with professional people that you really need to be on your side.

Philip: Working to get your Visas - no impact on me.

Lynne: I remember talking to Alex at the school and hearing about the rollercoaster of emotions you were going through...up one minute and down the next. A bitter disappointment re. the kayaking business...through the whole process again until Mike got the job.

DLD: I wondered how I too could become a reality show celebrity!!

Bob & Yvonne: We didn't really have much contact with Alex and Mike whilst they were going through the process of getting visas, so we did not feel or observe any impact. Listening to them talk about the process re-established our views of them, that they are a strong-minded couple who had the interests of their family at heart and were determined to succeed in obtaining and providing a better future for their family.

What was your reaction when you heard that we had visas and really were going?

David: Thank God he really is going!

Angus: Personally it was very sad to lose a family who we counted as genuine friends. Memories of lots of happy parties and laughter, crazy dancing by the children in the kitchen at New Year as we prepared food, lots of happiness and fun. So, to lose that was bad and it's always great fun to catch up with Mike and his anecdotes on his fleeting business trips back to the UK.

Mum: Pleased for you. It had been a hard slog and at last you could start making plans for packing up etc.

Dad: A big shock!

John: Given that reality had bitten so quick I felt you were acting too much on impulse and not enough on information. You were looking at a business which was very dodgy and I was concerned you were heading for trouble.

Richard: We knew that you were focused and determined to make this work and so when it all finally came right and the visas were issued, it was with an enormous sense of relief that your efforts had finally been rewarded, and sadness that you were actually leaving and taking your natural spark and energy away from the area, that we viewed this situation. You and the kids were always at the heart of things going on in the street and were the most generous in terms of your time and effort in making summer barbeques and parties a real street-wide occasion. Of course, we were envious too... we have often discussed with you our desire to do something more than just run our own businesses. Rosie's is a 7-day-a-week business and has made finding time to plan an overseas move difficult, due to the restraints it puts on days when we can attend meetings or exhibitions to find out more about relocating ourselves and our businesses overseas. We met you recently and discussed this, though, and it appears that we have now found a way to relocate to our ideal destination, one that is almost always hot, cosmopolitan, vibrant and unique in every sense. But enough about us...

Philip: When you said you were in New York on holiday I seem to remember (!!!) you were actually in New Zealand checking places out so didn't really know beforehand.

Lynne: Thrilled for you but sad too ☹

DLD: If I recall correctly, you were already on your way when we heard, but I had (and still have) great admiration for your commitment to actually go.

Bob & Yvonne: Well done to them, tinged with sadness that they were to be so far away.

Sister Les: Glad that it had turned out the way you wanted it to.

Sister Jake: Didn't really think about what you were going through, although sad for you when it didn't go as smoothly as you thought it would.

Were there any things you felt we could/should have done differently?

David: Done it earlier!

Sister Les: No

Mum: In hindsight I suppose going for a business took it out of you with all the disappointments.

Dad: Not really in my view.

John: I believe you should have avoided the "outdoor business" like the plague. It was not really viable, given the lack of information to base proper judgement on. Mike was always good at communicating with people and Alex so positive and dynamic, there had to be better opportunities and I am so glad you fell back on what you do best.

Richard: With the benefit of hindsight, it would be easy to say yes but when you look at how well you have all adapted to life in NZ it has to be said that the answer to this one has to be no. The trials and tribulations are what have made your physical move and your overall life journey so richly rewarding and entertainingly interesting. No doubt there are things that you look at and think "Wouldn't it have been easier if we'd only done....?" From our perspective, I don't think we are close enough to the day to day issues to say yes or no. Moving into rented accommodation obviously gave you flexibility to move quickly when the time was right but to many people this may have seemed a drastic step to take at a time when house prices were doing well and those extra few months would have seen your investment increase rather than paying out money on rent which was "dead" money. Having said that, we did a similar thing before moving to Essex to give us flexibility and speed when we found the right house so the decision made sense to us.

Lynne: Not really. We were surprised Mike took a job without having met the people with whom he would work and therefore no real security. The fact you made it work in spite of this is testament to your determination to make the move a success.

DLD: Gone ahead with the outdoor sporting business or at the very least bought a vineyard so we could all have had something interesting and enjoyable to do in our retirement (and drink even if we couldn't sell!)

Bob & Yvonne: No

Was there anything we did not handle very sensitively?

David: No, as MJC played rugby – hard, fast and direct!!

Sister Les: No

Sister Jake: How did we take the news of you going? Well we can remember the time you told us - by the pool on a glorious day, however, not because of your news but more because of ours. What was your reaction to ours? - you probably can't remember that was the day we had paid off our mortgage - a milestone for us boring old farts - hey but 2 bottles of bubbly was better than one. Could you have handled things more sensitively well in that instance yes - but then that wasn't anything to do with you moving! Other than that it was your decision to go and it was not our choice to disrupt your adventure.

Mum: Don't think so. You were living quite a distance away from the two of us and we didn't see all that much of you. With me not driving, I had to rely on Dad to bring me to see you, although I came up a few time by coach.

Dad: You hurt my heart but now 5 years on and being here and seeing your home and life you have all my blessings.

John: No, I don't think there was. After all, it was no one's business but yours and let's be fair, after the debacle of Equitable and the onset of a socialist government in the UK, a fresh start abroad was the best possible place to be rebuilding.

Richard: Not that I can recall but if it helps with a libel case or a personal injury claim, I'll have my lawyers let you know! In all seriousness, no. Your enthusiasm for this project and this move was infectious and whilst many people may have been ambivalent to the whole thing, we were overjoyed at your decision and progress throughout. We too share those feelings and see Great Notley as a transitory stage for us rather than a utopia type location in Essex from which we'll never move. There are too many small minded people who live small provincial lives and never dare to be bold or different and that attitude ensures that those who dare to move on with their lives will always be seen as mavericks and risk takers. It is a shame that people envy others rather than living their lives with similar energy and optimism. Sensitivity works both ways and people get jealous because they want more, envy others who take the chance when it's presented and then stay behind festering about life passing them by. They want it gifted on a plate and you and I know, Mike, that it's not that easy. If it was, we'd all be doing it but then if it wasn't hard, we wouldn't value it so much once we've strived to achieve it.

Philip: Sensitivity - once again no impact on us.

Lynne: Not as far as we were concerned.

DLD: Getting Bolshy when we insist that you cook! Reminding Mel that a woman's place is in the home! *[Footnote: I was very jetlagged, had a fair bit to drink and was being Kiwi, a tad direct, shall we say!]*

Bob & Yvonne: No.

How did you see our plans affecting the relationship we had with you?

David: I cried (with joy)!!

Mum: As long as we could keep in touch by phone and email. I know it was hard work for you when you first got there, but by heck, you soon got into the Kiwi lifestyle. Proud of you.

Dad: Alex was my eldest girl – when I moved from Greece I was single so less hurt. I was worried if I ever see my beautiful daughter again.

John: Apart from losing a couple of friends to nothing more than a few thousand miles in an ever shrinking world, it really had little effect.

Richard: Well, it was always going to make it harder to pop in for a beer and a bite to eat but actually we seem to be coping with that quite well on your frequent returns to the UK as the "Expat Guru". The world is a rapidly changing place and technology like Skype and obviously e-mail means that we are in touch regularly, albeit that with the time difference we are at opposite ends of the day to each other...you're having cocoa in your slippers at bedtime as we wolf down corn flakes in the morning before the start of our day. That said, the technology works and the video conferences on Skype are amusing and revealing, to say the least!

Philip: Relationship not affected. Over seven years ago we were on the course; you are the only one I keep in contact with.

Sister Les: Thought it would be nice to have family on the same side of the world as me.

Lynne: Although we hadn't been friends for that long, we knew we'd stay in touch.

DLD: Great! At least now we might now see more of you and perhaps even get a chance to come to visit you in NZ (really!)

Bob & Yvonne: We didn't think it would affect our relationship with Mike and Alex. If anything it has become stronger, we have more contact through e-mail now than we ever had before.

What was it like getting our letters in that first year – were they: 'welcome', 'informative', 'enlightening'?

David: Boring?

Mum: Very welcome and certainly informative.

Dad: Mum read letters - but meant nothing much as my head not in right place – still hurt.

John: I always felt quite excited for you when I got mail from you, it seemed as if you were in an "exploring" mood for quite some time.

Richard: More than that, they were witty, amusing, humble, real and touching. As you know, people are good at saying they'll keep in touch but the reality is very different. Your tenacity at keeping in touch is admirable and I imagine many people receive your emails and letters and read them with interest, laced with a touch of jealousy, and never take time to reply to them. We all live busy lives but, when we think about it, are we too busy to keep in touch with friends? We shouldn't be but does our obligation to employers override the time we should take to put pen to paper or to draft an email saying hi and how are you? All too often, I guess it does but then you'd be able to answer that better than we would.

Philip: The letters were very good. One thing I do remember thinking was, were you going to live there or was it just one big holiday?! Each text and email and letter seemed to build a picture of this perfect place, I remember the story you told me of the chap in the grocers who gave you a car!!!

Lynne: The letters were wonderful! It was lovely to hear about the journey there, the highs and lows and how you were all doing. Mike, you should write a book! (Oh, yes, that's right, you are!!!) Also, e-mail and MSN really help. Although the first time I saw little Gabs on camera made me cry as she had grown up so much.

Sister Les: Drove me mad at times - remember I'd done the same thing twice!

Sister Jake: Well the letters (by that I take it you mean e-mails) were interesting at the start - but now life goes on where ever you live you still have to eat, live and work and now life for you is the same for all of us.

DLD: Welcome, informative and enlightening even though they far exceeded Cookie's attention span.

Bob & Yvonne: The letters we received were amazing, very welcome, most informative and enlightening. Made us wish we were there.

Did the letters ever give you cause for concern?

David: You might be coming back!!

Mum: Well, naturally, as a worrier all my life, I just hoped you hadn't bitten off more than you could chew, but having been out to visit fairly early on I could see what a marvellous lifestyle you now have. Well done to all of you

John: When I realised you were struggling to get the business up and going, at first I was concerned. The fact that the children also took time to settle in made me think you were suffering more than you expected but fortunately all that was short lived and soon turned into success and more success. Once the children took over the mantle of "loving it there" for me that's when you really turned the corner.

Richard: Of course! Just because you're on the other side of the world, doesn't stop us being concerned about personal and professional issues affecting you. We all knew that this was going to be a challenging but ultimately rewarding process for you and so the ups and downs of daily life were always going to be exaggerated when you were away from your friends and family. Family health issues obviously had their role to play in this too and those times, more than any other, were deeply touching. Sharing those emotions and insights is not something everyone would want to do or indeed would have the emotional backbone to do. Your candour and openness is one of the things that makes you who you are and endears you to people. Others may find it intimidating because they are unfamiliar with this approach but that is their problem to address, not yours. The difficulty with being so far away is that all you can offer are works of support...the deeds that could have been performed if we were just round the corner were obviously much harder to offer and achieve.

Sister Les: No

Sister Jake: Cause for concern. Well you know the answer to that you originally said that you wanted to get off the treadmill and have more time for the kids and as you know from the many discussions you haven't achieved that aim and your kids and not going to be there for much longer.

Philip: Cause for concern not sure!!!! As above I did think how long will the honeymoon period last? It was all adventure although I wasn't in your shoes so I can't really say, did find the letters very informative. You probably don't need telling but put extracts of the letters in the book

Lynne: The only cause for concern was Mike's job especially when it didn't work out and you first set up BritsNZ. We worried for your financial security especially as Alex seemed quite 'low' at this time.

DLD: I was worried that you were naturally a little homesick but staying in touch with all your old mates on a regular basis must have ultimately made the transition that much easier.

Bob & Yvonne: No because they were honest and what shone through was the determination Mike and Alex had.

Did you at any time think/believe we would not succeed and did you at any time believe we would come back to the UK?

David: Never in doubt!!

Mum: Never, never, never, although Dad hoped you would.

Dad: Thought you might come back – I hoped you would! I did think though that you make it as you determined people, especially my daughter!

John: I was never sure, but I should have realised Mike and Alex don't give up easily on anything so I should have been more positive about it.

Sister Les: No

Sister Jake: There was no doubt in our minds that you would succeed because it seemed to us that there was no coming back for you - house prices going up , jobs not that readily available............and you do have some pride don't you?

Richard: No. This was never in question, you are not quitters, rather, we simply thought that you would come up with new strategies to overcome the difficulties you were facing. There were a few times when things were clearly rough and you would have been forgiven for throwing in the towel but returning here would have been an admission of defeat which is not your style. It is easy to say looking in from the outside as I am sure that there were times when that seemed like the only option but clearly it wasn't as you are all still there and thriving. The old adage of "When the going gets tough, the tough get going" isn't just a nice sentiment and a catchy tune, it's a fact of life with you that when things are difficult, you knuckle down together as a family and work through them. Too many people these days give up on important things without really making an effort to resolve them and address them. This is true of relationships, jobs, etc. You are made of hardier stuff than that and resilience, determination and a desire to the best for you and your family are all strong drivers and attributes that helped you through these tough times.

Philip: I never really thought you would come back to UK after tasting another life.

Lynne: No on both counts!! We knew you had steely determination!!

DLD: I was worried about your business on more than one occasion but ultimately believed that you would succeed and not return to UK. What is there to return to?

Bob & Yvonne: Never for one moment thought that Mike and Alex would not succeed or return to UK.

If you are aware that we have taken NZ citizenship what is your reaction to that news?

David: Poor Kiwis!

Sister Les: As I have duel nationality I always feel it's useful to have both also shows that you are acting in a positive way to the country you are living in.

Sister Jake: NZ citizenship if you are staying you should.

Angus: All I would say is that you and Mike are people for the moment and that may very well be the way to go I wish you all the success you deserve

Mum: Very proud of you all

Dad: It is good for your family. You can get into Australia easily and not bad to have 2 passports like me – UK and Greek!

John: As a family, New Zealand has done far more for you than the UK ever did or could, so why not. You are still the same people after all so what does it matter?

Richard: It makes perfect sense and proves that you are there for the duration! It is the ultimate statement to show that you are there and there to stay as well as saying to your adopted home country, we like it here so much we want to be a more intrinsic part of it...good for you. Many people will say, no doubt behind your back, that it shows a lack of respect to the UK and that you are turning your back on your home country. I think most intelligent people would recognise that the UK is not the country it used to be and nor do its values stand for what they used to. The pride has gone and our attempts to open our borders to everyone have backfired and seen our country become a multicultural mess because we've exploited rather than integrated those foreign nationals into our society. Bigotry and hatred fuel BNP rallies and politics and politicians fail to address the real issues affecting people so everyone becomes disenfranchised from UK PLC and simply looks out for themselves. There is a lack of sense of community and the same people who hide behind newspapers on their daily commute to the office, barricade themselves behind their doors when they get home and fail to communicate with neighbours. There is fear on the streets and our schoolchildren carry weapons for protection that actually cause provocation and a higher chance of them being killed or injured than our troops face in combat overseas. Is this the country you want to be associated with or would you prefer to live in a similar climate but with people who value family and friendship? Not much of a decision really, is it...sadly!

Philip: Citizenship - excellent news, what's that phrase; "when in Rome do as the Romans do" (maybe not. You know what I mean)

Lynne: We were really chuffed for you all. Again, it was testament to your determination that New Zealand was now your home.

DLD: Shocked that you could even consider supporting the All Blacks! Seriously though, Good on yer!! That is surely the final act of commitment and break with the past. In for a penny, in for a pound! I wish I could be so committed to being somewhere permanently.

Bob & Yvonne: In respect of the family taking New Zealand citizenship we think that is important. The family have started a new life over there and would wish to be part of the Country and community and what a better way to show the New Zealanders that you are totally committed to the country and integrating could there be? ....and finally, some thoughts from Alex's oldest and dearest friend:

Julia: I've been thinking a lot about when you left and everything you guys went through to get to NZ.

I think the main thing Jay and I felt about it was excitement for you and huge respect for this massive change you were making in your lives. You were never deterred by set backs that you had, in fact it seemed to make you even more determined!

Obviously at the time when you actually left I was in rather a bad state having only just lost my dad so that sort of overshadowed what I might have felt about you leaving otherwise. It feels a bit like a dream thinking back to that time.

I think Jay & I always felt that you & Mike would make a success of your move and knew a big part of that drive was to give your children a wonderful quality of life. We are so happy that it has all been such a success for you all!

Obviously the down side to your move is not being able to get together for a good old boogie!!

Footnote: *The David mentioned above is one of my oldest and dearest friends but you may be forgiven for thinking that with friends like that no wonder they left the UK!!*

Here we are at the last pages of our book. We trust that you have enjoyed reading it – and if we have written about anything and you are thinking "I wonder what happened…" Simply drop us an e-mail to info@britsnz.co.nz and ask!

We trust also that having reached this point we will have inspired you sufficiently that you will now grab the opportunity to turn your dream(s) into reality (no matter what country you are looking to settle in) and to potentially free yourself to do what it is you really want to do with your life(s)…no matter what it is that created that spark or what you do to maintain that desire just remember, we really do all have that power within, all we need is the belief and desire and of course the courage! You will NOT be "lucky" to be able to migrate – you will work real hard for that to come about but one thing you will need is courage…again we all have that within us too, so feel the fear but do it anyway as emigrating will change your life and the way you see it forever…and…if we can do it anyone can!

We would suggest that when you are sitting in old age with your zimmers around you it will be better to look back knowing you tried (and succeeded or failed, matters not!) than to look back and wonder!

In New Zealand you will find a society which has a really positive and forward looking attitude and which will simply encourage you to get out there and have a go…and talking with other successful migrants in Oz, Canada and USA they will say the same – working hard and succeeding are encouraged as is simply having a go!

Endings are always difficult and new beginnings can be scary, but more often than not soooo worthwhile so as us Kiwis would say:

You'll be right!

Some "locals" just out for a stroll – Taranaki is a huge dairy farming area and cows are clever enough to escape but not get back into the field – so on rural roads you "herd 'em up and move 'em out" to the nearest field!

MIKE, ALEXANDRA, JOSEPH, JACOB & GABRIELLA COLE

Proud to live and work in New Plymouth, New Zealand;

THE BEST CITY IN THE WORLD!

- Awarded First place and 2 Golds in the UN endorsed "International Awards for Livable Communities" (for cities of population up to 75,000).

- Awarded top city in NEW ZEALAND; North and South magazine, New Zealand 2008

"BRITS NZ - HELPING TO MAKE YOUR MOVE COMPLETE"

PSS International only do international removals which means that all members of their teams have been fully trained on export packing so that you know that your precious belongings are being packed by highly trained professionals giving your belongings the best protection as they follow you around the world.

Get PSS to quote for your move as soon as you can – ideally about four months prior to departure! Identify what you do not want to bring as early as you can – try selling your excess stuff and raise some money for your trip!

Ladies sit back and watch – for insurance purposes you can NOT pack anything yourselves and whilst this might be very frustrating it is important…as is a steady supply of tea for the "boys"!

NOTE
- Your container will probably be packed at your house on the back of a lorry.
- It will put down dockside in the UK
- It will be picked up and put on a ship heading to Singapore.
- In Singapore it will be put back on the dockside and the uplifted to another ship for more time at sea.
- When it reaches New Zealand it will be put dockside again and may be moved a couple more times depending on where you are in the country.

Given the amount of movement the container will go through it is amazing just how infrequently damage and breakage occur!

We are very pleased to have been associated with PSS over the last five years and highly recommend their services to you.

Halo Financial Services will look after all your currency needs in a professional and friendly way. They truly understand the emotions you will be going through and handle all enquiries speedily and fully.

We use Halo ourselves and have been delighted with the service we have received and it has been a pleasure to build a working relationship with them as we know our clients get great service and totally professional advice.

There are basically three ways in which Halo can help you trade:

- Spot Trade – buy now, pay now at the rate current at "this" moment in time.
- Forward Contract – buy now at the current rate, pay a 10% deposit and the balance at an agreed future date.
- Market Order – tell Halo the rate you want and the amount you want to trade and their systems will keep an "eye" open 24/7 and when the rate "hits" your target you buy at that level – this is an extremely good system to use when the markets are extremely volatile!

By signing on with Halo (which is free of charge) you will get access to a Broker who will give you a market view and can talk strategy with you.

As a Financial Adviser, Mike will also give you extensive advice relating to exchange rates and strategies and, most importantly, from the migrant's perspective!

345

The National Bank

We can highly recommend both these banks who both give excellent customer service and both of whom offer excellent internet banking platforms.

We use both banks ourselves both for our business banking needs and for accounts for the kids.

Both offer you the ability to open accounts in New Zealand before you leave the UK which is an absolute must do, as it makes your life so much easier on arrival in New Zealand.

Both banks have representatives based in London, both of whom are Kiwis, so not only can you get great advice on your banking needs but also a Kiwi's perspective of your new home!

More information about their services can be found by e-mailing us at info@britsnz.co.nz and put NZ Banks Accounts in the Subject line

"Outbound Media"

Providers of the new Emigrate magazine and organisers of the Emigrate shows in Edinburgh, Sandown, Belfast, Liverpool and Coventry.

We have worked very closely with these guys over many years both at the Emigrate shows and in writing articles in their New Zealand publications.

The publications offer a wealth of advice and articles about New Zealand and always include stories of those who have done what you plan on doing!

They do not only cover New Zealand – their publications also take in Canada, the USA and Australia and in our opinion are a MUST for anyone looking to emigrate!

As I have said they also organise the Emigrate shows and again for anyone looking to Emigrate these are a vital source of free, professional advice about your chosen destination!

You can find out more about them, their publications and the shows through their website at www.emigrate2.co.uk